Unfolding

Unfolding

A
High Holy Day
Companion

Rabbi
Karyn D. Kedar

CCAR
Press

REFORM JUDAISM PUBLISHING, A DIVISION OF CCAR PRESS
CENTRAL CONFERENCE OF AMERICAN RABBIS
New York · 2025/5785

Published by Reform Judaism Publishing, a division of CCAR Press
Central Conference of American Rabbis
New York, NY
(212) 972-3636 | info@ccarpress.org | www.ccarpress.org

Cover art: *After Light Darkness Rose 12*, copyright © 2025 Ellen Holtzblatt.
All rights reserved. Used by permission of the artist.

LIBRARY OF CONGRESS CATALOGING-IN-PUBLICATION DATA
Names: Kedar, Karyn D., 1957–author.
Title: Unfolding: a High Holy Day companion / Rabbi Karyn D. Kedar.
Description: First edition. | New York: Central Conference of American
  Rabbis, CCAR, 2025. | Summary: "Unfolding: A High Holy Day
  Companion invites readers into a contemplative spiritual exploration of
  the holiest months of the Jewish year. With each chapter, the reader is
  invited to linger on themes of beauty, memory, repentance, and
  forgiveness. A spiritual companion, offering meditations on a voyage of
  self-reflection, meaning, purpose, and love."—Provided by publisher.
Identifiers: LCCN 2024055276 (print) | LCCN 2024055277 (ebook) | ISBN
  9780881236668 (trade paperback) | ISBN 9780881236675 (ebook)
Subjects: LCSH: High Holidays. | Reform Judaism.
Classification: LCC BM693.H5 K43 2025 (print) | LCC BM693.H5 (ebook)
  | DDC 296.4/31—dc23/eng/20250107
LC record available at https://lccn.loc.gov/2024055276
LC ebook record available at https://lccn.loc.gov/2024055277

Cover design by Barbara Leff

Text design and composition by
Scott-Martin Kosofsky
at The Philidor Company, Rhinebeck, NY
www.philidor.com

Printed in USA
10 9 8 7 6 5 4 3 2 1

To my ancestors:

Alta, Nellie Weisman, Evangeline Dion Schwartz,

and my brilliant mother,
who died as I was writing this book,

Lynore Ray Schwartz

. . . a matriarchy of wisdom.

All existence whispers to me a secret:
I have life to offer, take it, take it.
—RABBI ABRAHAM ISAAC KOOK

Contents

THE TEN DAYS OF REPENTANCE
The Broken Heart, the Injured Spirit

YOM KIPPUR
Returning Home: Forgiveness and Repentance

Return Home: Character and Moral Compass

Return to Love

Gates, Books

Reckoning

Acknowledgments

To EZRA, my husband, who understands my primal need to write and never complains when our dining room table transforms into an altar of creativity covered with paper, colored pencils, books (the kind with a spine), candles, a computer, cups of coffee, water with lemon, an evening gin and tonic (always with lemon, never lime), and scraps of this and that for months on end. Your understanding sustains me through the chaos of creativity.

To Talia Shaked, Shiri Bar, Ilan Kedar—my children, my thought partners, and my loves. You are brave, brilliant, and beautiful. I have so much to tell you and learn so much more when I listen to your ponderings. I have much admiration for the people you have become.

Creating a community of sustainers is everything—people who see you, who hold you in your silences, who comfort you in your despair, who celebrate with you, and who let you be, just as you are. You are a diverse group of people, my motley crew, and I appreciate you all. Thank you to Barbara and Rick Silverman for offering your corners of beauty for me to write and think, for gently asking how it's going, and for reading an essay here and there.

A writer's posture is sitting, bent in thought, shoulders feeling the world's weight hunched for long hours. Thank you, Kyle Danielson, for being my partner in health. Reaching, bending, lifting, pulling, and stretching all helped me find my balance. Without tending to my body, I could not have dwelled in my creative mind.

Thank you to Linda Sivertsen, who skillfully led the Beautiful Writer's Retreat, bringing together a small group of women who formed a circle of trust and encouragement, all within a short walk of the powerful Pacific Ocean. We spent five days writing, reflecting, and sharing. Stayed tuned—the next book has begun.

To Christina Haas, my writing sister—your gentle, affirming, and wise spirit is a source of support and inspiration. Thank you.

Thank you to Lisa Howe and Scott Stavrou, the brilliant facilitators of Write Away Europe. In the peaceful beauty of a Tuscan villa surrounded by vineyards, lavender, olive trees, and laurel, you provided the perfect space and environment for creativity to flourish. Ladders of holiness . . .

Thank you to Rabbi Amy Scheinerman, who graciously read early versions of this book.

To my publisher, CCAR Press, thank you for continuing to believe that my offering is a worthwhile endeavor. Thank you, Rabbi Hara Person, chief executive of the Central Conference of American Rabbis, brilliant friend who is tirelessly working for the Jewish people—all the time. Thank you to Rafael Chaiken, director of CCAR Press, who continues to grow the catalog, giving voice to this generation of authors with a small but dedicated staff. Dear Rabbi Don Goor, you are a kind person and a talented rabbi with a diverse set of skills that you use for the greater good. To Raquel Fairweather-Gallie, thank you for making us visible. Deborah Smilow, thank you for keeping the wheels greased. To Debra Hirsch Corman, eagle-eyed copyeditor, Michelle Kwitkin, excellent proofreader, Barbara Leff, gifted cover designer, and Scott-Martin Kosofsky, creative designer—thank you all. Thank you also to Ellen Holtzblatt for creating the beautiful art for the front cover of this book.

To Rabbi Anne Villarreal-Belford, a gifted editor. You understood my cadence and voice and guided me with incredible skill and compassion. Thank you.

Introduction

The Rhythm of the Calendar

IN 1905, Chayim Nachman Bialik published a long, powerful poem called "The Pool." My favorite verse is "... when I was young and my days were sweet, and the wings of the Presence first rustled over me, my heart knew longing and amazement and I sought a secret place of prayer."

I wish I could remember where I was when this verse found me. Long before I found the words, their meaning was already my companion. I remember the wooded walks of my youth—it seems I was born a seeker. I would linger long hours in the mystery, writing even then, with every word, every turn of the phrase serving that mystery. It still does.

My wondering is my prayer. Beauty is my prayer. My spiritual agitation is my prayer. My prayer is the quiet by the window, which frames my thinking room as the sun sheds an early hue. I have sought silent amazement all the days of my life. I linger.

And I invite you to linger with me. This volume is my attempt to synchronize our spiritual search for meaning with the heartbeat of a few weeks of the Jewish calendar. It is an ode to our mortality, a song to our sense of impermanence. The words are meant to scratch at our imperfections. If we are flawed, and we truly are, then what is our worth? How do we find our purpose within the cracks and fissures of our being? Where do we find meaning?

We live and tarry in these questions for just a few weeks, from Av to Elul to the beginning of Tishrei. This becomes an arch where we slowly become aware, touching our existential longing to live deeply, intently, lovingly, and meaningfully. It is an invitation to a spiritual unfolding.

We begin with Tishah B'Av, the ninth day of the Hebrew month of Av—a time of mourning and remembering the many calamities that have befallen the Jewish people. The month of Av is a solemn period grounded in historical circumstances that encourages deep personal reflection. The Temple was destroyed on the ninth of Av in 70 CE because of human frailty; we chose hate over love, and all was lost for the nation. So too, with us—when we give in to negativity, we lose so much. Destruction, we learn, is caused by senseless hatred. Redemption will come with love.

We begin here, in the ashes, for we learn from our tradition that we are but dust. We are of the earth and will return to the earth. This is not a statement of self-deprecation—after all, we are also taught that we stand on holy ground—but rather a call for a humble perspective. It is the reality of human nature to rise and to fall, to love and to hate, to give and to withhold. The month of Av grounds us with a simple warning: Humanity has the unlimited desire and capacity to create and love, but at the same time, humanity has the will and the means to destroy itself. Av asks us to dwell in our desire to live an elevated life—an unfolding toward loving rather than fear.

Nestled between the lowliness of Av and the overwhelming spirituality of Tishrei is the ethereal month of Elul. Elul invites us to contemplate thoughts of forgiveness, love, and beauty. For the entire month, we sing songs of penitence, praying. Praying that we will be forgiven, for we are deeply flawed. Praying that we can forgive, for we are afraid to let go. Remembering that we are created for glorious things—if we can live a life of strength and resilience, depth and compassion.

Love is not a feeling but a spiritual state, not an emotion but a practice. We yearn for an expansive love that lifts us and connects us to our highest impulses. To be gentler with ourselves and find greater self-love. To embrace our relationships with open hearts and understanding. To find a faith grounded in the awareness that love abides and abounds if only we reach for it.

The mantra of the month of Elul is Psalm 27, recited daily: "There is only one thing I seek, to gaze upon beauty all the days of my life" (verse 4). We consider words and concepts such as God, holiness, love, and beauty. For me, they are synonymous and the dwelling place of the aspirational soul.

The calendar leads us further into the thicket of reflection, self-awareness, moral accountability, and spiritual elevation. The first ten days of the month of Tishrei are called the Ten Days of Repentance. For weeks now, we have readied ourselves for the intensity of these ten days. We have practiced sustaining a thoughtful and contemplative pose, thinking about where we have come from, who we are, and who we desire to become. We have tended to our wounds, nurtured our hearts, and immersed ourselves in matters of the spirit. It is healing to realize that these days begin with Rosh HaShanah, a celebration of Creation, when the world shines new and we know that the power to recreate ourselves lies within our attention and intention to do so. The shofar sounds, a clarion call to awaken what lies dormant within so that we may journey ever deeper into repentance and forgiveness, unfolding into a deeper sense of self.

And then Yom Kippur. We are tired, humbled, ecstatic with hope, crying out one last time. We deny ourselves food and drink. On this holiest of days, with nowhere to go, we go inward. We use metaphors that create a sense of urgency like "the gates begin to close" and "seal us in the Book of Life." We sing one more time of sin and repentance, rocking ourselves, hopeful that we can find the way, the path to a deeper life. A more thoughtful life. A forgiving life. And we bring our generations with us, immersing ourselves in loss and memory and the acute understanding that we are mortal. Morality is the demanding consciousness of Yom Kippur, bidding us to live better, deeper, and kinder. From dust. To dust.

This Book as Spiritual Grounding

You may want to follow the journey of the calendar and read this book in a linear manner, one page at a time, beginning at the beginning and progressing day by day. Or you may want to read it the way I wrote it, from the middle out, flipping through the book and allowing a passage to find you. And once it does, pause and let the words be your companion throughout the day. Think and feel its truth as your spirit perceives it. There is no beginning or end to the spiritual journey; instead, it is like a spiral, twirling and whirling, wondering and wandering through the complex landscape of our inner life.

This book is an invitation to pause, reflect, and unfold. We so rarely find time and space to linger and tarry by the window of contemplation, once again getting acquainted with the complexities of our inner lives.

This book invites you to find a quiet moment, just a moment, and enter the pages. Maybe as a bedside companion coaxing your sleep to journey with you as you examine the obstacles, paths, and byways that lead you deeper into self-awareness. Or maybe with a cup of tea in the early morning before the hustle and bustle, before the noise and distractions, before the day takes hold. A morning moment of reflection.

This book is a series of prompts for conversations with the Invisible or with friends, considering the many soulful aspirations such as a sense of purpose, hope, personal heroism, and meaning. And repentance and forgiveness. And love and kindness. And beauty—we so want to dwell in beauty.

This book is deeply personal; I have always said that we teach what we need to learn. I often write in the first person, with the belief that though our biographies are different and our stories are profoundly diverse, we share a yearning and striving to find meaning in our complex lives, to live with less conflict and greater connection, to self-actualize, to live a life of purpose, to love and be loved. We all share the pursuit of a deeper understanding of ourselves, our relationships, our faith, and our place in the world.

This book is an unfolding of the complex landscape of the inner life. It names the struggles we all have as we reach toward a meaningful life, the sometimes harshness of the journey, and the aspirational triumph of having walked the path.

When we weave together stillness, intention, and practice, then something shifts. When we are not afraid to say we are sorry, when we find a path to forgive, then something shifts. When we unfold into the pursuit of a deeper understanding of ourselves, our faith, and our place in the world—when we become seekers—something shifts. Every day has the potential to be a powerful day. Imagine embracing the themes and metaphors of this season, lingering in longing and amazement and the deepest questions of life. Imagine unfolding.

One page at a time.

A Note on Translations

My translations throughout this volume are poetic ren-
derings. I am in dialogue with the original text, using it
as a platform for inspiration and creative interpretation,
embracing artistic freedom. All the sources are cited, and the
Hebrew text is frequently included so the reader can track my
work and enter into their own dialogue and understanding of
the source material. When I use other translations, they are
cited. With a few exceptions, I have changed the pronouns to
provide a more inclusive tone.

Av

Humble Dust
Fertile Ashes

Comfort, comfort oh My people, says your God.
—Isaiah 40:1

Lofty Thinking

I ASK YOU TO JOIN ME as we aspire to lofty thinking, to a transcendent love affair with the all-pervasive beauty in life. I ask you to choose hope. To believe in what is possible, despite what seems probable. At times you refute and in exasperation you say, *But Rabbi, hope is not a strategy.* But I reply, almost in a whisper, *Hope is the most compelling of strategies.* Indeed, it is through the propelling power of hope that we see our way out of stagnation and constriction. Hope is not about a future plan; it is about expansive thinking in the present. It is the spiritual principle that makes sense out of life when it is chaotic and overwhelming, the answer to despair and confusion.

> So, I pray with the psalms—
> I cry out to You, oh God, I have felt constricted
> and constrained. Help me lift my eyes to the
> mountains, to the heights, to the vastness of
> possibility and to the vistas of an open heart,
> to the awareness of abundant beauty.
> Majestic is the presence of God, the
> heavens are covered with splendor.
> Lessen my fear that I may live
> within Your love, hopeful,
> grateful, and
> forgiving.

Down to the Foundations

TELL ME OF YOUR BRUISED HEART, battered soul, and the dings and dents of the spirit. We all have a story to tell. Me, as well. Details come in flashes of memory, and often memory is not a reliable reporter. But the spirit is. We walk among the ruins of an inner landscape, a tender child, wanting to be loved, to be visible, to be known. Reflecting, fragile, vulnerable. Hurt causes us to be afraid and fear, sometimes, makes us behave badly.

So we must begin here. We sit a while to remember. We linger here because what happened then, happens now. To me. And you too, dear reader.

And in the dust and ash of long ago, we find fertile ground from which to grow even stronger. And I believe with all my heart that a difficult memory can teach resilience, and a softened heart can learn forgiveness, an awakened spirit can practice repentance.

I am but dust and ashes, and the world was created for me. This is the paradox of the spiritual unfolding. I want to practice unfolding within the contradictions.

We begin here.

The Story Is Told:
Love Builds, Hate Destroys

TWO STORIES are the foundation of our collective consciousness; they are the bedrock of our belief system, parables with a singular message. One story recounts two men who hate each other. The parable has a pointed message: Senseless hatred destroys and, indeed, is the reason for the destruction of the Second Temple and our exile from our land. The other story is about two cousins who love one another selflessly and unconditionally. This parable, too, has a pointed message: Love builds, and the very spot of their embrace and loving tears is the spot where the Temple is built. The Temple is built on a foundation of love and is destroyed on the foundation of hate.

A TALE OF SENSELESS HATRED

RABBI YOCHANAN said, "What is the meaning of the verse: *Happy is the one who lives with awe, but those who harden their heart shall fall into harm*"?

Once there was a certain man whose friend was named Kamtza and whose enemy was named Bar Kamtza. This man decided to prepare a large feast. He said to his servant, "Bring me my friend Kamtza." The servant went and mistakenly brought him his enemy, Bar Kamtza.

The man hosting the feast came and found Bar Kamtza sitting at the feast. He said to Bar Kamtza, "Why are you here? What is it that you want? You are my enemy. Arise, and leave right away."

Bar Kamtza told him, "Since I am already here, let me stay. Do not embarrass me by sending me away. I will give you money for whatever I eat and drink." The host said to him, "No, you must leave."

Bar Kamtza told him, "I will give you money for half of the feast; do not send me away." The host said to him, "No, you must leave."

Bar Kamtza said, "I will give you money for the entire feast; do not humiliate me, just let me stay." The host said to him, "No, you must leave."

Finally, the host took Bar Kamtza by his hand, stood him up, and took him out.

Jerusalem was destroyed on account of Kamtza and Bar Kamtza.

—Based on Babylonian Talmud, Gittin 55b–56a

A TALE OF ABUNDANT LOVE

TWO COUSINS lived on opposite sides of a mountain. One was rich but had no children, and the other had many children but was very poor.

The rich cousin thought, "I have so much, my cousin has so little; let me secretly cross the mountain at night and bring my cousin extra crop." The poor cousin said, "I derive so much happiness from my children; let me secretly bring some of my crops so that my cousin could have a little extra joy in this world."

And so it went: Every night, each cousin secretly crossed the mountain to bring the other food. Every morning, the cousin would inspect their stock to learn nothing was missing. Neither could explain the phenomenon, but they thanked God for kindness and continued their goodwill.

After years of this routine, there was a shift in the timing. Instead of missing each other at night, the cousins met on top of the mountain. Surprised, they looked at each other and suddenly realized what had been happening for all the years. With great love and gratitude, they embraced one another on top of the mountain. They cried for joy, realizing that their love for one another was so deep.

The place where their tears fell became a holy place, the foundation for the Temple.

Hate or Love

I DON'T THINK that I have ever hated with a baseless, senseless hate. But I have senselessly obsessed over hateful things—like the many betrayals of trust, dignity, fairness, and equality I and others have suffered. Playing the scenarios over and over again, in my dreams, with a friend, alone with my thoughts. A senseless obsession that would cause me to spin as if I were caught up in a tornadic waterspout. I hated that.

I don't think that I have ever loved without bounds, completely to the core boundless love for its own sake. No expectations, no boundaries, no criticism, no holding back, pure vulnerability, always raw and true, deep and constant like the underground rivers that circle the planet. That kind of love. If I were to be honest.

We can practice hate without bounds, unconditional, baseless, hate for its own sake, or love without bounds, unconditional, abundant, love for its own sake.

It is down to the foundations, foundational, with profound simplicity. I have a choice. We have a choice. Hate or love with reckless abandon and then live accordingly.

> Sister, run to me in the cover of night
> so that we may embrace and cry
> and fall upon the mountaintop,
> first sobbing, then gently weeping,
> then quietly in love.

The Story Is Told:
The Ruins of the Temple

ONCE, RABBI YOCHANAN ben Zakkai and his student
Rabbi Y'hoshua
walked among the ruins of Jerusalem.
There was stillness, an eerie silence.
They entered the holy Temple, and even the boulders
were smoldering.

Rabbi Y'hoshua grieved and cried in anguish—
"This place, this sacred site, has held the
offerings of our hearts as
we atoned for all of our wrongs,
for the sins we have committed.
It now lies in waste, destroyed,
the hope of our spirit is in ashes."

Rabbi Yochanan ben Zakkai turned to his student,
eyes kind yet stern.
He said, "My son, do not grieve.
When we do not have the altar of God
to atone for our wrongdoing,
we have another way to repent from our sins."
"And what is that?" asked the student.

"Deeds of love and kindness," said the teacher.
"Love and kindness."

Acts of Love and Kindness

WALKING AMONG THE SMOLDERING ASHES, two friends paused. They journeyed from the north of Israel to return to Jerusalem after having escaped the utter and complete destruction of the Second Temple by the Romans in the year 70 CE.

I imagine their silence.
I imagine their attempts not to give in to despair.
I imagine the weight of leadership upon them and
I imagine they understood
that the survival of the people was like embers in the ashes;
it could reignite or grow cold in the destruction.

I imagine that it was in a barely audible whisper that Rabbi Yochanan ben Zakkai said to Rabbi Y'hoshua:
This was the place of holiness, where we came to atone for our sins. Where shall we go, how shall we repent?

Rabbi Y'hoshua answered:
Acts of love will redeem us. Kindness will atone for our sins.

How is it that love was the answer? They had been through a war of a conquering army. This army took prisoners from their homeland and sold them into slavery in Rome. The place in which they expressed their spiritual survival through elaborate rituals of sacrifice was destroyed. And yet, atonement would come through acts of love.

Atonement comes through acts of love.

The Story Is Told: Resilience

The landscape of the Western Galilee of Israel is soft and beautiful, where abundant rainwater makes the green hills fertile. I look up to the mountain slopes at the terraces created by farmers centuries ago. There are pomegranate and fig trees, mulberry bushes, and grapevines.

Underground streams flow near caves and are a common place of refuge. After the Roman destruction, Rabbis and their students took refuge in these mountains to answer one abiding question: How do we go on in the face of unspeakable tragedy?

RABBI Y'HOSHUA SAID:
My sons,
come and I will tell you.
Not to mourn at all is impossible,
because what has happened has been decreed.

He said:
My daughters,
come and I will tell you.
To mourn too much is impossible,
because the Sages will not impose a decree that cannot be endured.

Rather,
thus say the Sages:

A man may paint his house,
but he should leave a corner bare,
so that all may see.

A man can prepare a banquet,
but he should leave out certain foods,
so that all may know.

A woman shall adorn herself with jewels
but leave out a stone,
so that all may understand.

Not to mourn at all is impossible.
We suffer such great loss.
But let us not fall into darkness as we remember our loss.
To mourn too much is to deny the power of the spirit.

We shall once again sing songs of praise.
We shall once again dance with joy.

—*Based on Babylonian Talmud*, Bava Batra *60b and Psalm 137*

ELUL

The Dawn Breaks

The best time to recite S'lichot *is just before morning*
called ashmoret—*the last watch—of the night,*
a time of mercy and acquiescence,
a time of anticipation for the dawn of new light,
a time to hope for the revelation of God's word in the world.
—P'ninei Halachah, Days of Awe 2:6:2

Forty Days

IN THE VERSE "I am my Beloved's and Beloved is mine"
(Song of Songs 6:3), we find a secret, hidden meaning. The
first letters of each Hebrew word spell *Elul*, and the sum of
the last letters of each word have the numerical value of forty.

This teaches us that there are forty days
from the beginning of Elul to Yom Kippur.

> Forty days to return,
> to repent,
> to open up your heart.
>
> Forty days to
> approach the Beloved
> with a contrite heart.
>
> Forty days to soften,
> to become more loving.
>
> Forty days
> to feel the acceptance
> of the Beloved.

אֲנִי יְשֵׁנָה וְלִבִּי עֵר
קוֹל דּוֹדִי דוֹפֵק
פִּתְחִי־לִי אֲחֹתִי רַעְיָתִי.

I was asleep, but my heart was awake.
My beloved knocks, and I say,
"Open my sister, let me enter my beloved."

—Song of Songs 5:2

A Knock on the Door

הַשְׁמִיעֵנִי בַבֹּקֶר חַסְדֶּךָ
כִּי־בְךָ בָטָחְתִּי
הוֹדִיעֵנִי דֶּרֶךְ־זוּ אֵלֵךְ
כִּי־אֵלֶיךָ נָשָׂאתִי נַפְשִׁי:

As the dawn breaks,
I shall hear Your loving presence.
I trust You to help me
understand the road I must travel.
I lift my weary soul.

—Psalm 143:8

I BEGAN TO DOZE in the sunlight of a chilly morning in Mexico. I was sitting on a windowsill bench with a notebook, colored pencils, and a computer nearby. I was teaching at Rancho La Puerta about the spiritual principle of love. In between classes I wrote, inspired by the crisp mountain peace.

On the plane to Mexico, I read an article in *Poets & Writers* magazine by Melissa Burkley. She describes a phrase in French literature—*entre chien et loup*—which translates to "between dog and wolf." It is the time of day when the light is such that we cannot distinguish between the two animals. In Rabbinic literature, this time of day is dawn. When light banishes the darkness and we *can* distinguish between wolf and dog, we know it's time to sing of unity and recite the *Sh'ma*. But in French literature, the time of day is dusk, when the dark banishes the light.

Writers and other creatives relish the state between sleeping and waking. This is the place where discernment lives and creativity flourishes. In the article, Burkley tells the story of

Edgar Allen Poe sitting in a chair with a coin in his hand and a metal bowl on the floor. He would doze off, his hand would relax, and the coin would drop on the metal bowl, making a sound and waking him up. At that moment between sleep and waking, he felt he was his most creative, and he would then write.

So, I nestled into the windowsill cushions, letting my eyes close. Listening to the quiet, my breath. In and out, until I began to doze. My chin fell forward, waking me. I grabbed my computer and began to write:

> *Make your prayer tumble*
> *like sagebrush driven by the wind*
> *any wind here and there*
> *circling with dirt and dust*
> *down a quiet road.*

Tumbling between "dog and wolf," when the waking mind is fuzzy and the wistful heart alert, I tumble through prayer.

Once, when I was a young bride, my husband and I stayed at his parents' small Jerusalem apartment. We slept on a couch that opened to a full-size platform bed. The bed was very firm, the room small, the night restless. It was a warm early September, the Hebrew month of Elul, weeks before Rosh HaShanah. I had finally fallen into a sound sleep when a sharp noise woke me up. Men were pounding on the doors all over the Jerusalem neighborhoods, shouting with urgency one word over and over: "*S'lichot, S'lichot.*" They called out, rousing households from their slumber to join the neighborhood minyanim in prayers of supplication and repentance.

"What is that?" I asked my husband. "Sephardic Jews say the predawn prayers of *S'lichot* every night in the month before Rosh HaShanah," he said. "Ashkenazic Jews say *S'lichot* prayers only on the Saturday night before the holiday.

My father rises every night before dawn during this month to pray." We fell silent; he turned over and fell back asleep. But I watched the shadows dance and sing upon the walls in joyful poignant prayer.

Between dog and wolf: A place in the shadows, in the quiet road of tumbling, deepening, pondering, questioning. I rise. There is a knock on the door.

W HEN YOUNG RABBI ELEAZAR *of Koznitz, Rabbi Moshe's son, was a guest in the house of Rabbi Naftali of Roptchitz, he once cast a surprised glance at the window, where the curtains had been drawn.*

When his host asked him the cause of his surprise, he said, "If you want people to look in, then why the curtains? And if you don't want them to, then why the window?"

"And what explanation have you found for this?" asked Rabbi Naftali.

"When you want someone you love to look in," said the young rabbi, "you draw aside the curtain."

—Martin Buber

The Days of Awe and Terror

The line between awe and terror is just one breath's
width away.
The sentence can be the medium that can transform
awe and terror into a kind of meaning.

—Ocean Vuong

I am my Beloved's.
Beloved, are You mine?

Why is this day called both awe
and terror?

Are You my Beloved?
I am Yours.

And the deer prance.
And the gazelles leap.

And lilies are beautiful
this time of year.

And I wander in the fields looking for my Lover.
I am in awe of the greatness and grandeur and vast
exquisite expanse.

And terrified,
lest I be lost and never found among the roses.

I know now,
I am small, a speck of golden dust only seen in
Your ray of light.

I am Yours, Beloved.
Be mine.

Shedding a Skin

1.

On a Wyoming mountaintop path, across from the
Grand Tetons, I walked and I listened.
Below, in the valley's bed, I saw the great and powerful
Snake River curve and flow.

I felt, in that moment, that I was being called to worship.
Compliant, I stood still for a long while,
and the Snake River
was quiet and I was quiet and the air was quiet, still.

I watched the grasses along the slope stand straight,
soft, and tall.
Their slight crimson stalks pointed to the heavens
proclaiming their beauty.

I looked up and saw, in the broad daylight of the
midmorning sky,
the half-moon of Elul, tilted, spilling out in urgency
as if to say:

> *We are called to attention. Pay attention.*
> *These days are precious.*
> *Now is the time to change, transform, unfold.*
> *The majesty of the river flows, nothing stays the same.*
> *It is time to shed the old habits and assumptions that*
> *keep you from beauty such as this.*

2.

So I wondered what it feels like when a snake sheds its skin.
Does it hurt like the ripping of a bandage?
Does it feel light and clean like the first haircut of
the summer?

Is there sadness and loss?
Or does it feel oddly free of old and familiar constraints?

What does it feel like when that snake forms a new skin?
Does it prickle and sting?
Does it itch like the healing of a wound?
Is there a sense of awe at the newness of it all?
Or fear that the new will not be as comfortable as the old?

3.
And the mountains and the valleys and the river and the sky.
And the snakes and the grasses and a woman
wandering a mountaintop path.
And the sounds and silences and the need to change
and the resistance.

> *Let nothing stay the same. It is time to shed the old*
> *habits and assumptions that keep you from beauty*
> *such as this.*

The Inner Life: Cheshbon HaNefesh

לְךָ אָמַר לִבִּי בַּקְּשׁוּ פָנָי . . .
My heart has said to You: "Seek my presence."
—Psalm 27:8

THE INNER LIFE is complex and complicated. It is a paradoxical landscape that is hard to decipher and yet so familiar—magnificent but confusing. An unattended field that has been neglected, ignored, and forgotten. The place where I feel lost, the place where I feel found.

It is home; I live from the inside out. Here rests the narrative of my life, my stories, and my memories, the many promises and aspirations of my soul. Here live my pain, my fears, and an obstinate character that resists change.

I go inward and tread upon the sprouting weeds, wildflowers, and grasses. Each step animates grasshoppers, gnats, and flies that sting the ankles, bite, and buzz. Each step shows me what it means to be in awe of the beauty, of the occasional butterfly, glorious and free. Each step brings me closer to understanding and self-awareness.

How I long to be glorious and free—free from the fears that make me behave badly, free from guilt, free from anxiety, free to be authentic, earnest, and loving.

"The King is in the field, the King is in the field," proclaims the Alter Rebbe. It is Elul, and God has left the palace, no longer on the elusive and distant throne in a faraway palace, surrounded by moats and guards. *Royalty is in the field, the Eminence is in the field*, and I run to greet the majesty as I search for meaning, for purpose, for my essential self.

Elul. I shall tend to my inner life.
Elul. And reckon with my human frailty.
Elul. I walk in a fertile field of longing, of belonging.
Elul. Reach for me, O Transcendent Force, and I shall be tender and gentle. Make my small and simple life grand and expansive, as large as the horizon of possibility.

I am in the field to greet You. Where are You?

A Word

*A person awakens their innermost thoughts and draws
the truth from their heart through the power of the
words of their mouth.*

—*Sefer HaChinuch* 606:2

WE BELIEVE WORLDS are created and destroyed by the
words we speak. In our morning prayers in the section called
P'sukei D'zimrah, we chant in positive affirmation, *Blessed
is the One who spoke and the world came into being*. Through
the power of the word, God created the world, and light,
and goodness, and blessing. Even *Aseret HaDib'rot* (the Ten
Commandments) is more accurately translated as "the Ten
Utterances."

Words we say to others and words we say to ourselves shape
us, create our identity, and form our self-image. Notice how
you describe yourself to yourself. Caring, honest, ambitious,
adventurous? Driven by a sense of service to the greater
good? Driven by relationships? Curious? Sometimes mean?
Angry? Sad? Bored? Bored with the same conversations
over and over again? Bored with the daily routine? Bored
with your job? Uninspired? Or inspired? Inspired to make
a difference in this world, to help, to create, to help others?
Content? Present? Loved? Every word matters.

Words and phrases you heard as a child—*you can't, you
shouldn't, how dare you, who do you think you are?* And worse.
Phrases that have become an internal monologue of self-
deprecation, a habit that makes us believe in limitations that
are of our own making.

And the words of praise, positivity, and possibility expand the boundaries of who we are and what we can achieve.

Every New Year, I choose a word to carry with me as a companion, a word to contemplate, like "patience," "grace," "kindness," or "presence." I write it down on several scraps of paper and place it in strategic spots, like the bathroom mirror, the refrigerator, or near my favorite chair. With a regular glance, a word like "confidence" or "compassion" or "willingness" would teach me, inspire me, remind me.

Some years I used it as the screensaver for my computer, so when I paused in my work or while writing, a word like "forgiveness," "grace," or "presence" would float by. And when a word like pause or notice or generosity would arise in conversation or while reading, I would understand its impact on my life just a bit better. And knowing the Hebrew of your word adds a different dimension. For example, "patience" in Hebrew is *savlanut*, which means "bearing the burden of others"; this adds depth to the understanding of the word.

Listen to your inner voice and expand the vocabulary one word at a time. A word of intention. A word of kindness, a word to motivate and soothe an anxious spirit. A word to consider and contemplate.

שְׁמַע־יְהֹוָה קוֹלִי אֶקְרָא וְחָנֵּנִי וַעֲנֵנִי:
אַל־תַּסְתֵּר פָּנֶיךָ מִמֶּנִּי אַל־תַּט־בְּאַף עַבְדֶּךָ
עֶזְרָתִי הָיִיתָ אַל־תִּטְּשֵׁנִי וְאַל־תַּעַזְבֵנִי אֱלֹהֵי יִשְׁעִי:

I call out, hear me, answer me, do not hide.
I ask for grace. I ask for Presence.

—Psalm 27:7, 9

A Question

I'VE ALWAYS BEEN DRAWN to the magnetism of the desert. The paradoxes of an inhospitable beauty, of stark possibility, of the need to get lost, to be found. And the silence. Many types of silences, and multiple ways to hear, to listen. Silences that sting and swat my restless mind. Silences that open my heart, teach me how to breathe, and throw me into the wild practice of discernment. Silences that invite me to live within questions. No answers.

The power lies with the question, not with the answers. It is true that the answers are satisfying. They are like a bench alongside the path where we can sit a while with a sense that the journey has a resting spot. But in truth, the journey of the spirit has very few moments of pause. There is always another question, something more to understand, another dilemma to grapple with, more steps that will lead us to greater meaning. A good question invites us to embark on a quest. It propels our journey toward self-discovery.

What are your questions? Don't begin with the word "why." There is no good answer to "Why?" Every question that begins with "why" has an answer that is unknowable—why did she have such a hard diagnosis, why do good people suffer, why is there evil in the world? Rather begin with "how" or "what." How can I find a greater sense of peace? How can I be of service? What is my next active step? What do I need to understand to find my purpose?

Toss your question out to the universe without regard for the answer. I call this "playing catch with the universe." Live within the question, linger in the thought. It may take a few days, a month, or even a year, but the answer will come to you. Have patience.

This, after all, is the season for questioning.

Self-Reflection

ONE EVENING, over the summer, the humidity was thick and heavy. Clouds rested upon the horizon, obscuring the sunset. I wanted to see the colors—brilliant, morphing, illuminating the point where heaven met the earth. But it was not to be. Even still, I sat a long while watching.

The sailboats were turning to come back to the harbor, one after another, majestic beauty gliding on the still waters of the Mediterranean Sea. I was at a seaside restaurant. I ordered a chocolate mousse cake with caramel sauce and took a few bites. I sipped strong coffee over ice.

And I sat.

I sat for a long while.

It was the month of Elul, and I was in a state of sustained contemplation. I knew there was meaning in this moment, but I had no words to explain what or how. There was something about the tarry—watching the clouds, the invisible setting sun, witnessing the return to harbor.

This is how it is sometimes. Once, my friend proclaimed, "I want to become a human being rather than a human doing." We practice self-reflection when we allow ourselves to linger. Not everything is immediately clear. When I got up to leave, I carried with me a sense of peace. And today, right now, we are in preparation for the Days of Awe.

> Change happens in slow increments of pause.
> These are days of self-reflection,
> when, despite the ordinary day,
> we declare it a day of awe.
> How I love to tarry in the ordinary.
> Waiting to notice what begs to be seen—

like the sweetness of a piece of cake,
the heat of the day,
and the safe return to harbor.

The return to safe harbor.

The First Day of Fall

I STOOD SMALL on the shores of String Lake
lifting my eyes to that holy place of
cloudy skies and mountain peaks.
I crawled into my heart
moving aside the hubris
that comes from fear.
Smaller even still.

It is a lifelong nudge—
each requires a unique
consideration:
The moving.
The hubris.
The fear.

Let it be said,
that only here, here, in the contrast
between the majestic mystery of autumn
and the ego that won't let go, can we learn
to be small.

Today is the first day of fall.
Let fall away what no longer serves us,
fall away the fear, fall away the self-doubt,
fall away the terror that comes from
not feeling love, not being in love, fear
that we may never adequately be loved.

Nonsense. It is reckless not to rehabilitate.

For what is love if not the healing force of time
that leads us to the water's edge of soul-adjusting beauty.

The learning it takes to become small inside, a heart that knows the truth
that love overflows abundantly when we step aside from our fears,
onto the shores, peaceful and content with our small place in the world.

Rosh HaShanah

The Mystery
Prayer, God, Silences

Bless me, my spirit
with tenderness instead of might!
. . .
Tenderness, you ineffable name of God,
be my image of God!
—Rabbi Abraham Joshua Heschel

The Marshlands of Prayer

at first

the language of supplication is foreign
the language of prayer is inaccessible
the language of God is unknown
the language of devotion is lofty
the language of repentance is perplexing
the language of poetry is bewildering

puzzled

I sit a long while
the pieces begin to form a picture

like a herd of wild mustangs avoiding roundup
like locusts hatched from the trees after a
seventeen-year sleep
like a flock of a hundred thousand starlings flying in a
mysterious murmuration
like seven hundred emperor penguin chicks jumping off a
cliff in Antarctica

like a solitary soul making her way through
the marshlands of prayer

PraiseSong

הַלְלוּ־יָהּ
הַלְלוּ־אֵל בְּקָדְשׁוֹ
הַלְלוּהוּ בִּרְקִיעַ עֻזּוֹ:

הַלְלוּהוּ בִגְבוּרֹתָיו
הַלְלוּהוּ כְּרֹב גֻּדְלוֹ:

הַלְלוּהוּ בְּתֵקַע שׁוֹפָר
הַלְלוּהוּ בְּנֵבֶל וְכִנּוֹר:

הַלְלוּהוּ בְתֹף וּמָחוֹל
הַלְלוּהוּ בְּמִנִּים וְעֻגָב:

הַלְלוּהוּ בְצִלְצְלֵי־שָׁמַע
הַלְלוּהוּ בְּצִלְצְלֵי תְרוּעָה:

כֹּל הַנְּשָׁמָה תְּהַלֵּל יָהּ
הַלְלוּ־יָהּ:

HALLELUJAH.
Praise the Divine in sacred places;
praise the Divine in the mighty heavens.

Praise the Divine for powerful deeds;
praise the Divine for boundless greatness.

Praise the Divine with blasts of the horn;
praise the Divine with harp and lyre.

Praise the Divine with timbrel and dance;
praise the Divine with lute and pipe.

Praise the Divine with the sound of cymbals;
praise the Divine with loudly with t'ruah.

With all our breath, praise God.
Hallelujah.

—Psalm 150

LIFE IS LIVED IN HARMONY and dissonance. Sometimes everything seems so right, and sometimes nothing makes sense. Sometimes I live high, and sometimes I live low. I come to these days anxious, in anticipation of some magical shift. But how?

Am I brave enough to hold myself accountable? I will pray. For hours, I will sit in prayer. Pray on it, my friend, the evangelical pastor would say. Pray on it.

Prayer is a solitary fight at dawn, as quiet as a thin whisper of sound, lingering in the mind like residue, a remnant of dark wanderings. My way to sincere prayer is a slippery path, elusive, evasive, often too subtle for words.

This Book of Prayers is written in metaphor, giving voice to my desires through poetry and song. Sometimes, the words seem off; the metaphor does not fit my theology or my sense of God. Sometimes, the words frighten me, and I argue with them. But still, I pray.

Sometimes, I wander away from the book, distracted. I make lists in my head of things I should do, and that, too, drifts away. I begin to daydream. Then, I am drawn to the din of others praying. I love that rumble and tumble sound, muttering intention. I notice the man next to me cast in a spell. He has been lulled to sleep by this sound. His wife is embarrassed. His is a sacred sleep that only the heart hears.

When you don't know what to say, when you don't understand what is being said, sing.

And let your song lift you. Sing like the clashing cymbals, like blasts of the horn, sing aloud or sing in your heart, sing with words and sing with melody. Your song is your prayer, and your song is your intention.

And when you simply cannot sing, breathe. Your breath is the life force. Your breath is your prayer. Your breath is your intention. Follow your breath. Sit quietly and let the sounds wash over you. You are here, present in the mystery, surrendering to the ineffable.

Trying to be. Trying to be. Let it be. That, too, is my prayer. The delicate release of judgment, fear, and anger will open the gates of prayer. Wordless, wonderful, letting go.

Hallelujah.

The Unknown

Alone I sat next to God
who lost me in the wide spaces
like a piece of sky
and never came to look for me.
—Rivka Miriam

I DON'T THINK that God hears our prayers. Not in the way my father heard my cry late at night when the shadows made me nervous and I wanted to feel his loving presence, his smell, and his kind eyes one last time before I surrendered to the dark. I called out for water and he came.

Not so with God, though I have been known to call out to the Invisible—a fleeting, ambiguous Presence. How can I pray to You when I am so unsure? My prayer is an exclamation point, and more often, it is a question mark. It is the guttural sound of despair and defiance. It is a sigh—a deep, soul-wrenching, wordless sigh.

There is so much talk of God. I don't know God, but let not my unknowing be a barrier to prayer.

Who can really know just about anything? This is the truth. There is a dangerous chasm—call it melancholy, call it the place where meaning cannot exist, call it chaos, or even worse, call it apathy—between what we can know and what we will never know.

We sit here today, today on the holy days, to tend to what we can possibly know through hard work and contemplation. How to be kinder to ourselves, how to help others, how to find forgiveness, how to make a difference in a world that sometimes appears indifferent. It is hard to know these things—it takes work, practice, serious contemplation, and more contemplation. But they are in our reach. That is why we sit here today, on the holy day.

And there are things we will never know. Why is there so much suffering? Why do good and evil tussle, and evil often wins? What is God, after all? Who shall live, and who shall die? All this is in the realm of mystery. Today, we admit that there are things that are simply unknowable, and we are learning to accept the mystery of it all. That is why we sit here, today on the holy day.

I am learning not to resist what I cannot understand, what I will never know.

Do not resist. Not knowing is humility, I say. That, too, is prayer, I whisper.

This is the moment for uncertainty.

I will only resist the existential fall into despondency.
I will not turn away even as Your Presence has left me alone and lonely.
I know so little, so very little.
That too is a prayer.
My prayer.

So, dear God, would it be okay if tonight, on this holy day, would it be okay if
I called out to You in the dark?

This is why I am here today.

Clarity

I HAVE SQUANDERED the early hours with thoughts
blank as the page before me.
It's been quite a wordless wandering.

It is a peaceful meandering to feel the hours settle upon
a turquoise velvet couch and then contour into a
sedentary stance.
To let the eye gently gaze with astounding humility
and to forgive my persistent clenched jaw
and to notice that a periodic sigh
is breath.

And then to finally stretch, sip strong coffee,
slightly sweetened
as the day is slightly sweetened, becoming stronger from
wordless persistent thought and an honest mingling
of sadness and joy, my heart holding
what words
cannot.

And then finally this—
a poem or a prayer, a simple nod to a moment,
suspended above the cares of the world.

Nevertheless, let me be clear.
I ask only this:
to see beauty,
to dwell in beauty,
to be beautiful.

Never
the
less.

Hannah's Prayer

She stood alone in a far field, bent over, rocking ever so slightly. Her lips moved, but there were no words. She cried and she sobbed, but there was no sound. Her heart poured out to God. She was immersed in anguish and distress. Misunderstood, she was close to despair.

I see you.
I hear you.
I believe you.

Quiet Down

WE NEED SOLITUDE to quiet down.

Only here do we hear the murmurings of our soul.
But we don't flourish in isolation.

We need acceptance so that we may grow and evolve safely.
But we can't live an expansive life if we are resigned to the
   way it is.

It is hubris to think we are the only ones searching for
   meaning, seeking purpose.
We live in community, in proximity to others—
   neighbors and seekers.

Invisible as we may feel at times, we are not alone.

WHEN A PERSON tries to pray but struggles to lift their voice with melody, and then another person comes along and raises their prayer with song, then the one who struggles finds the strength to sing. This shared moment is the secret bond between spirits.

          —Martin Buber, "The Rung of Love"

Avinu Malkeinu

WE SAY *AVINU MALKEINU* again and again, traveling the spiritual terrain of mixed metaphors and paradoxes, the experience of God pulling us close, pushing us away.

Linguistically, *Avinu,* "our Father," and *Malkeinu,* "our King," is a mixed metaphor—"Father" is ever so familiar, "King" so distant and unapproachable. Spiritually, *Avinu Malkeinu*—our Father, our King—is a paradox. Sometimes, God is like a wisp of knowing, sometimes an incomprehensible mystery. Sometimes translucent light, sometimes opaque and dark.

Are You *Avinu,* or are You *Malkeinu*?

You are distant and remote, like a faraway star whose radiance cannot be seen. You are the turbulence sending me asunder, tossing my heart to thoughts of death. You are the deep purple velvet cape of a Monarch, glimmering as the light catches when You pass by. You are on the other side of a moat, high on a mountaintop, surrounded by guards who keep me away. You are silent, grand, out of reach.

Are You *Avinu* or *Malkeinu*?

You lift me, carry me like a precious bouquet of flowers. You tend to my tears, bandaging my wounds. You speak to me in soft tones. You care for me and feed my soul. You are kind. You comfort me when I go astray and teach me to stay away from danger.

Are You *Avinu* or *Malkeinu*?

You scare me with Your stern reprimands and confuse me with harsh reproach. There is so much I don't understand, so much of the time. Why do some suffer? Why do I suffer? Do You hear my prayer?

Are You *Avinu* or *Malkeinu*?

We speak a human language of metaphor and symbol. Words dance around my existential questions. Images that try to capture our experience of some unknown, unknowable transcendent power. Translucent light, opaque—You are neither *Avinu* nor *Malkeinu*, though sometimes I feel that it is so.

You live in my contradictions, hover in the creases of my paradoxes. You dwell in the blind spot of the soul.

You who are here, You who are nowhere—*choneinu vaaneinu*, be gracious unto me, hear my prayer.

Hin'ni: *Here I Am*
The Confession of a Broken Heart

I AM HERE.
I am here.
I stand before the open ark and
the eternal scrolls of our people
dressed in white light.
I stand ready to enter the Holy Days,
to offer prayers that urge me
to live better, kinder,
ever present to the pain of others,
to become a vessel of compassion, trustworthy,
holding hope in the midst of despair.

Hin'ni.
I am here, I am here.
I stand on the edge between earth and heaven,
between what I know and what I can never understand,
between life and life everlasting.
Mortality hovers, a rippling presence,
always there—lingering, waiting, holding.
I am here.

Hin'ni.
I am here.
I stand resilient, determined,
though I have been taken down,
forced to live a different way.
The rhythm of life has been altered.
Time unfolds and morphs, expands and stands still.
I have been called to be present, to pay attention.
What I have I learned?
What have I done with the time I have been given,

glorious time of never-ending possibility?
Have I squandered the beauty, the radiance of life,
an offering to my inner being?

Who am I?
Where have I gone astray?
Am I worthy to pray with my people?
May I be worthy to pray with my people.

Hear my plea,
grant me the faith, courage, and wisdom
to enter into *cheshbon hanefesh*:
the fragility and humility of self-examination.

Hin'ni,
I am here, I am here.
May this fractured heart soften
and hold love and compassion
in a way it never has before.

Hin'ni, I am here.

Proclaim the Power of This Day:
Un'taneh Tokef

LET US PROCLAIM *the power of this day, for it is awesome*
   and full of dread.
On Rosh HaShanah it is written; on the fast of Yom Kippur,
   it is sealed:

How many shall pass from this world,
How many shall be born into it;
Who shall live and who shall die;
Who will reach the ripeness of age,
And who will be taken before their time;
Who by fire and who by water;
Who by war and who by beast;
Who by famine and who by drought;
Who by earthquake and who by plague;
Who by strangling and who by stoning;
Who will rest and who will wander;
Who will be tranquil and who will be troubled;
Who will be calm and who will be tormented;
Who will live in poverty and who in prosperity;
Who will be humbled and who exalted.

But through return to the right path (t'shuvah), *through prayer*
(t'filah), *through righteous giving* (tzedekah) *we can transcend
the harshness of the decree.*

Who shall live and who shall die, I do not know. But I know
that somebody will and that, someday, I will.
   Where will this moment find me when I look at the Angel
of Eternity eye to eye? Walking by the way, when I lie down
or when I rise? Surprised or at peace, afraid or undisturbed,
victim or serene? I do not know. I cannot choose.

Trust me, oh my soul, that I will settle into the long shadows unafraid, for Thou art with me.

I have practiced all the days of my life to speak plainly in prayer and sit with stillness in supplication and gently implore the Invisible. I have practiced how to lift my hands to the heavens and touch the edge of mystery unafraid, daunting as it may be. I have practiced not knowing why. I do not know why. Why do people suffer? Why is there evil in this world? Why some by fire and some by wild beast? I have practiced being a sister to the mystery.

Where will this moment find me? I do not know. But in the confusion and sometimes in the despair, in the beauty and sometimes in the awe, I have learned that the practice of generosity is an art and that graciousness is a cultivation. May this moment find me in deep embrace as another trembles, giving away kindness freely, and a dollar or a sandwich, a pair of socks or a warm coat, the humble touch on the shoulder of one who feels unseen. In passionate pursuit of peace. Peace. Loving mercy and justice all the days of my life.

I do not know where this moment will find me when I come face-to-face with the Angel of Eternity. But I know it will. I will return to the Source having practiced repentance. A thousand ways to say I am sorry. To bow my head and kneel. To ask forgiveness again . . . and once again. To listen to the burden of another without comment.

Less judgment, more curiosity. There are a thousand ways to return home to the solace of innocence, humility, unknowing, unafraid, caring more, listening more. A thousand ways to return. To turn away from sin and turn toward love. Let the moment find me well-practiced in the return to love.

Who shall live and who shall die, I do not know. But I know that somebody will and that, someday, I will. May a life of prayer, *tzedakah*, and repentance find me soft and strong when the Angel of Eternity reaches for me, touches me on the cheek, and takes me home.

The Story Is Told:
Find the Aspirations of Your Heart

AFTER HIS PRAYER, Rabbi Alexandri (though some say it
was Rav Hamnuna) would say:

> May it be Your will that You place us in a lit corner and not
> in a darkened corner, and do not let our hearts become
> faint nor our eyes dim.

And Rabbi Elazar would say:

> May we rise early and find the aspiration of our hearts.

—Based on Babylonian Talmud, B'rachot 16b–17a

Hide and Seek

For the sin we have sinned before You unwittingly;
For the sin we have sinned before You willing;
For the sin we have sinned before You deliberately;
For the sin we have sinned before You secretly;
For the sin we have sinned before You openly;
For the sin we have sinned before You knowingly;
For the sin we have sinned before You unknowingly;
We have sinned in all of these, as it is written:
Concealed acts concern Adonai, our God (Deuteronomy 29:28).
Except for You, we have no one who pardons and forgives.
        —*Siddur Rav Amram Gaon*, ninth century

WE CAN'T HIDE. We try all the time. Adam, eating the fruit
of the most beautiful tree in the garden—a tree called knowing—becomes afraid, stripped down, naked, and vulnerable.
So he hides. And God seeks. And in this brief poetic exchange
between the first man and his Creator, we are drawn into an
eternal game of hide-and-seek.

We are so afraid of our faults and inadequacies. Our imperfections terrify us and strip us of our confidence. We feel
unsafe in the presence of others. We hide from each other.
We try not to reveal our true selves, nor say too much, nor
become too vulnerable. We feel like imposters because there
is often a gap between what others see and what we know to
be true. We are imperfect human beings in a daily struggle to
be good enough, smart enough, and giving enough. Enough.
So, like Adam, we hide.

We hide from ourselves. How little do we know of the complex and gnarled byways of our psychological lives and how
they intersect with our spirit and, ultimately, our purpose for

living? We simply are a mystery to ourselves, and even if we step upon a path of self-discovery, the treasures buried deep within are uncovered slowly, bit by bit, over many years. I am a work in progress, we say. But mostly, we hide.

Cowering in the thicket, in a garden east of Eden, we pretend not to hear the presence of a commanding force, a loving presence that transcends all that we know and understand, that tugs us toward eternity and holiness and goodness. That reminds us that beauty redeems and love heals all wounds. Like a wisp of wind, God calls us to remember what we have forgotten, that we are loved and that love heals all wounds. And that there are consequences to our attitudes and actions, words, ungracious whims, carelessness, and callousness. We are unaware of the impact of our words and actions, so we unwittingly offend and unnerve one another. We pretend, and we hide.

But the game is hide *and* seek. So, during these holy days, if not before, we engage and try to emerge from our hiding place into the light, asking for forgiveness, even if we don't know we did wrong, for we have done wrong.

A MOMENT AGO a tear came down my cheek,
I was afraid you didn't love me.
Then I remembered,
Of course you do.
My fear makes me forget.
My tear lets me remember.

—Rabbi Sheila Peltz Weinberg

The Story Is Told:
The Whole World Is Full of Glory

"WHERE IS the dwelling place of God?"

This was the question with which the rabbi of Kotzk surprised a number of learned people who happened to be visiting him.

They laughed and responded: "What a thing to ask! Is not the whole world full of God's glory!"

Then the rabbi of Kotzk then answered his own question: "God dwells wherever we let God in."

—Martin Buber

Where shall I find You?
Your place is lofty and secret.
And where shall I not find you?
"The whole earth isfull of Your glory!"

. . .

I have sought to come near You,
I have called out to You with all my heart;
and when I went out toward You,
I found You coming toward me.

—Judah HaLevi

In Common

Each of us has a name given by our sins and given by our longing.

—Zelda

WE WALK THROUGH THIS WORLD feeling invisible, acting invisible, and sometimes trying to disappear. We keep to ourselves, keep our distance, and are careful not to overshare. We drive through rather than linger at a café. We make plans months in advance instead of crossing the yard or going down the hall and knocking on the door of our neighbor to have tea or wine before dinner. We keep our heads down as we walk through the office, the park, the crosswalk. We are quiet, or we talk a lot about a lot of nothing. We have forgotten how to listen. To be curious. We judge. All the time.

There is a sustained invitation to step out of the shadows of invisibility and stay a while in contemplation, revealing to ourselves, and perhaps to another, our regrets and our loneliness, our search for love. An invitation to notice where we stand in this world and what we stand for.

We are about to be called to come back. Back together out of our isolation, into community. Communing, gathering, and sharing deeply what we all have in common are the fundamentals of our humanity. We share so much. We may not know each other's name, or if we do, we may not know each other's story. But we do know this: We are all yearning for love, tending to our sadness, and struggling with loss. We all have the desire to share our joy and our exuberance, to dwell in beauty, to find meaning, to have a purpose in life. All of us want to make a difference. To matter before we die. That is why community has its roots in the word "common." The stranger is not so strange after all.

A synagogue is called *beit k'neset*—the home in which we gather—the place to collect ourselves in the company of others. To think and soften our hearts and expand our minds and listen and be heard, and be of help, and to be helped. We gather because we want to belong to something beyond ourselves. We are not meant to live alone. And yet we are oh so lonely. We gather so that we no longer feel invisible.

Now is the time to offer a safe and gracious space for ourselves and for others where we can consider our stories. A sort of show-and-tell. There is understanding in the telling; let there be revelation in the revealing, and forgiveness in the recounting. The poet says, *Tell me about despair, yours, and I will tell you mine.*

I ask only to
be named, to be noticed, to be known.

Call me by my name and you have my attention.
Notice when I am here and when I'm gone and you
have my loyalty.

Know me, see me, hear me, and you have my heart.
Ask me to help, and I will extend my hand.

ROSH HASHANAH

Wandering, Wondering

וּמֵאֲרָצוֹת קִבְּצָם מִמִּזְרָח וּמִמַּעֲרָב מִצָּפוֹן וּמִיָּם:
תָּעוּ בַמִּדְבָּר בִּישִׁימוֹן דָּרֶךְ עִיר מוֹשָׁב לֹא מָצָאוּ:
רְעֵבִים גַּם־צְמֵאִים נַפְשָׁם בָּהֶם תִּתְעַטָּף:
וַיִּצְעֲקוּ אֶל־יְהוָה בַּצַּר לָהֶם מִמְּצוּקוֹתֵיהֶם יַצִּילֵם:
וַיַּדְרִיכֵם בְּדֶרֶךְ יְשָׁרָה לָלֶכֶת אֶל־עִיר מוֹשָׁב:

Redeem us from adversity,
gather us
from east and west,
from the north and from the sea,
we have lost our way in the wilderness
and found no place to rest,
our spirit fails,
we cry out in our affliction,
rescue us from our sorrow,
lead us to a place to settle,
guide us to safe harbor.

—Psalm 107:3–7

A Thousand Sparks of Light

I AM A THOUSAND SPARKS of light
and have traveled an ancient distance
of time and space.

I am connected to the Source.

I am a thousand sparks of light
carried upon waves of darkness—
chaotic void.

I am in formation.

And every day
I am invited to listen
for my calling

to be
and to do
and to create
and to love
and to forgive
and to remember

that I have traveled
a great distance
to be called

to say yes to life.

The Empty Chair

IF WE ARE TO BE SAVED then it is by beauty.
By quiet thoughts and stormy reflection
and sustained moments of contemplation.

By the tickle and tackle of the muse.
By reading poets and philosophers,
by the melodies and song,
by a splash of color or simple black and white and gray,
by movement, disciplined and free.

And by nature. Nature is redemptive.
The mountain reach, the wooded path, the secret spring,
the flicker of light and shadow upon the leaves, the sun
rising, rising, rising upon the horizon or behind the cloudy
cloud, the knowing light within the darkened sky, the moon
hidden, new, full, disappearing yet again, the ice, the storm,
the perfect temperate day.

And the sea, which rocks us like our mothers once did,
holding us tight through their exhaustion and fears,
humming, quietly singing. That sound, that embrace.

And if we are to be redeemed then it is by longing
to return home, back to simplicity.
And by accepting the invitation
of an empty chair to tarry by an open window.
And in the quiet moments
finding our way to an open heart.

If we are to be saved.

Dwell in Beauty

אַחַת שָׁאַלְתִּי מֵאֵת־יְהֹוָה
אוֹתָהּ אֲבַקֵּשׁ
שִׁבְתִּי בְּבֵית־יְהֹוָה כָּל־יְמֵי חַיַּי
לַחֲזוֹת בְּנֹעַם־יְהֹוָה
וּלְבַקֵּר בְּהֵיכָלוֹ׃

Just one thing I have asked of God,
only this do I seek,
to dwell in the house of God, all the days of my life,
and to behold the beauty of holiness
and to frequent the palace of the Divine.

—Psalm 27:4

WHAT ARE YOU GOING TO DO? she asked.
I am going to step into the expanse of my life, I answered.

There is beauty in the sublime, there is beauty in the mundane, he added.
Show me, I said.

You have found it, they said.
Behold—you dwell in the beauty. That is the expanse of your life.

Simplicity

שֹׁמֵר פְּתָאיִם יְהֹוָה דַּלוֹתִי וְלִי יְהוֹשִׁיעַ:
שׁוּבִי נַפְשִׁי לִמְנוּחָיְכִי כִּי־יְהֹוָה גָּמַל עָלָיְכִי:

God protects the simple; I was downcast, God is my salvation.
Return, O my soul, be at rest, for God has been good to you.

—Psalm 116:6–7

SIMPLICITY,
beautiful maiden,
you are the soul sister of my elusive muse.
Draw me near to your abiding presence.
And teach me the art of constancy to
the essence of your being.

Longing and Amazement

When I was young and my days were sweet
and the wings of the Presence first rustled over me,
my heart knew longing and amazement
and I sought a secret place of prayer.
——Chayim Nachman Bialik

LONGING.
A curious state,
a spiritual statement.
At first, longing seemed restless,
a soulful wandering through angst and sadness.
Didn't the world understand?
And then

amazement

Religion consists of
God's question
And our answer.
        —Rabbi Abraham Joshua Heschel

To Consider

WE ARE ASKED
to surrender
to the softness
in life
where love
is abundant and
faith is our guide
and forgiveness is our path.

We examine
ourselves and
ask the hard questions,
those silent ones
that direct our soul
and our spiritual path.

We check
our relationship
with God and
have a conversation
that is honest,
direct,
imploring.

We honestly consider
our relationships
and ask for forgiveness.
We offer forgiveness.

Let us answer the call
to review,
redirect,
and renew
our determination to live a life where love is abundant—
a faithful life.

The Story Is Told:
Lost and Found

HANOKH OF ALEXANDER taught:

One day, there was a simple man who, each morning, had a difficult time remembering where he had left his clothes the night before. So one day, he got a pencil and a piece of paper and wrote down where he was placing each article of clothing. He placed the note next to his bed and thought to himself, "Tomorrow I will have no trouble finding my clothes!"

He woke the next morning, quite pleased with himself, took the note, and followed it to the letter, finding each piece of clothing exactly where he had set it down. Within a short period of time he was completely dressed.

Suddenly he was seized with a terrible thought: "But where am I?" he cried. "Where in the world am I?"

He looked everywhere but could not find himself.

"And so," taught Hanokh of Alexander, "so it is with us."

Rosh HaShanah

The Names of Rosh HaShanah

וְאָמַר סֹלּוּ-סֹלּוּ פַּנּוּ-דָרֶךְ הָרִימוּ מִכְשׁוֹל מִדֶּרֶךְ עַמִּי:

God says:
Build up, build up a highway, clear a road.
Remove all obstacles from the road of My people.
                              —Isaiah 57:14

Keep me from all that I might comprehend!
O God, I ripen toward you in my unknowing.
                              —Rachel H. Korn

The Names

Rosh HaShanah is known by five names.
  Rosh HaShanah: The Beginning of the Year
  Yom T'ruah: The Day of the Joyful Blast
  Yom HaZikaron: The Day of Remembering
  HaYom Harat Olam: The Day Before the World Is Born
  Yom HaDin: Judgment Day

How many names do I have?

The one who begins again, over and over.
The one who sings loudly with joy, sometimes like a lion and sometimes like a jackal.
The one whose memories she cannot leave behind, like a soft carpet, or a bed of nails.
The one who is waiting to be born; the one who is judged harshly, kindly, and all the time.

The one who unfolds like the days and the nights and the irises reborn in spring—blue, blue, blue—one beautiful moment at a time.

The Hidden Moon

Between Rosh HaShanah (Kese) *and Yom Kippur* (Asur)
we cast away the evil inclination,
* justify us in judgment so that the light of life shines on us.*
Behold we have come to You, Mighty and Glorious One,
for with You is the source of life, in Your light shall we see light.
                              —S'lichot Nusach Ashkenaz Lita 9:2

THE MOON IS NEW, a soft silver light, barely visible. It is
a new month and a new year. It is Rosh HaShanah, the
beginning of the Ten Days of Repentance.

Oh, hidden moon, you cast but a shard of light, reflecting
the secrets of my heart. I ask to be good, to do good, and to
have goodness enliven my life.

Oh, tender moon, you announce a New Year, a celebration
of Creation, an invitation to walk a correcting path—a path
of beauty, humility, radiance, and reflection, just like you.

Oh, reflective light, I too am a reflection of my hopes and
dreams. I reflect upon the hidden places within me, the dark
corners, the unknown barriers that keep me from my full
potential. Answer my plea.

What holds me back? What keeps me small?

Potential is a beautiful sight, bright and illuminating
against the dark, like the vision of the willing soul, ready,
anticipating.

The Story Is Told:
Carry the Light Within

A YOUNG RABBI complained to the rabbi of Rizhyn: "During the hours when I devote myself to my studies, I feel life and light, but the moment I stop studying it is all gone. What shall I do?"

The rabbi of Rizhyn replied: "That is just as when a person walks through the woods on a dark night, and for a long time is joined by another, lantern in hand, but at the crossroads they part and the first must continue on alone.

"But if a person carries their own light with them, they need not be afraid of any darkness."

—*Martin Buber*

HaYom Harat Olam:
The Day Before the World Is Born

Today the world is born anew.
This day, the whole of Creation stands before You
*   to be judged.*
As we are Your children, love us the way of mothers
*   and fathers.*
As we are Your servants guide us by the light of Your
*   justice, grace, and holiness.*
                    —From *HaYom Harat Olam* liturgy

WITH THIRTY-TWO WORDS in Hebrew, this unknown poet creates a poem with expansive metaphor and concise language. The world is conceived (*harat olam*) and held in mercy like a mother holds her unborn child in her womb. And the Hebrew word for the world, *olam*, is also the word for eternity. This holding, this pre-Creation moment, is the ultimate meaning of Rosh HaShanah for the poet. We are at once grounded in time and space. We are here now, asking to be held in mercy. And we are somehow in an eternal state of potential and perpetually filled with possibility.

And it is the shofar, a wordless exclamation of sound and memory that summons our labor. We can do good. We can do wrong. Held, hidden away, about to be born anew, we listen to the blasting sounds and shake off the complacency that restrains us. We feel the sound's vibrations releasing our negative preconceived notions of who we are and what we are. We bear the burdens of our life, heavy and sad.

And if we are to be judged, let it be gently. We are but children in our spiritual evolution. The years have not yet made us wise. We ask to be judged with compassion. We are but servants of the Highest Good, trying to deepen our dedication to justice and kindness.

Hayom harat olam, let this be the day we are born, recreating ourselves in the image of our secret dreams. Glorious. As the poet says, our world is held in merciful light waiting to be released.

Yom HaDin: *The Day of Judgment*

All of humanity passes before the Holy One for
judgment on Rosh HaShanah.
                    —*Mishnah Rosh HaShanah* 1:2

MY THOUGHTS AND HEART are consumed with capturing moments of holiness. Is it the same for God? All words we use to describe the spiritual experience of the sublime are metaphors, approximations of our sense of transcendence. I do not believe in the God of reward and punishment.

I prefer a gentler experience of the Divine. These are
   my theological similes—
God is like love and beauty and grace and song and
   wholeness and compassion.
These are the words I use as synonyms to describe my
   ethereal experience of the Ineffable.

So, this Day of Judgment is a Day of Spiritual and Moral Reckoning. And we all need moral reckoning.

We have all but banished the word "judgment" from our vocabulary and societal norms. We try not to be judgmental of others, not to judge ourselves. But there is right and wrong. There is good and evil. And sometimes we choose poorly. We suffer from a lack of good judgment. And often, we find ourselves in an ambiguous space that asks us for moral discernment. But do we sit awhile in discernment? Do we ask for clarity in conversations with the closest of friends?

We need Rosh HaShanah as *Yom HaDin*, the Day of Judgment. Today, we are acutely aware and held accountable for our deeds, decisions, excuses, and inaction. Our *machzor*, the High Holy prayer book, is heavy with words and lists of the myriad ways we have spoken and acted wrongly, neglected and ignored paths of peace.

Do not confuse judgment with shame. Shame diminishes our love and life. It puts us in the shadows, cowering, hiding, and loathing. Judgment is like a compass. It responds to the magnetic field of moral and ethical behavior, guiding us and pulling us out of the shadows to follow the north star of human decency, virtue, and righteousness. The ancients who formed the Hebrew language believed in this connection: The Hebrew words for conscience and north share a linguistic root, *tzadi-pei-nun*. May our conscience be our guide.

No shame. Rather judgment, discernment, and repentance are part of a lifelong process: an awareness of our behaviors and intentions, acknowledging them aloud, asking for forgiveness, and then correcting course.

K'dushat Levi softens the word "judgment" even further by noting that the Hebrew root *zayin-mem-reish* means "to sing" and also "to prune." Sing, sing songs of praise. And let your song prune away what can no longer live. Cut away the brittle branch so that we may flower and bloom. For we are song and we are gardener, so let our deeds be as a melody to holiness and our words blossom with kindness.

These Are the Days of Awe

THESE ARE THE DAYS OF AWE, the Days of Judgment.
O, Eternal Source of peace, hear our plea.

Judge us, inspire us, compel us
so that we will not turn away—
never to be silent, never to be numb,
never to be distracted, never to let our bewilderment
and exhaustion keep us from
doing what is right, what is good,
and what is demanded of us, O God,
to love mercy, pursue justice, and walk humbly.

These are the Days of Discernment,
the Days of Self-Examination.
God of compassion and love, hear our prayer.

Give meaning to our confusion, purpose to our pain,
and bring healing to our fragmented hearts.
May our tears ease the suffering of another.
When we love our neighbor, we transcend;
when we love the stranger, we transcend;
when we do not stand idly by, we transcend;
when we pursue peace, we transcend;
when we hold the world as a vessel of grace, we transcend.

These are the Days of Renewal, the Days of Life.
Divine Source of good, hear our heart's desire.

Lift us, guide us, command our eyes
to gaze into the shadows, and upon the streets,
and into every place that evil strays and preys
upon all that is good and beautiful in our world.
Send us forth, that we may be Your servants,
choosing blessing over curse, bearing witness.

May we proclaim from the heights and from the depths
the power of goodness, beauty, righteousness, and hope.

These are the Days of Holiness and You are the Holy One
of Blessing.
We will not tire, we will not despair, we will not turn away.
You, dear God, are the Source of peace in the high heavens.
We are the source of peace here, upon the earth.

ROSH HASHANAH

Shofar
Breaking Through Complacency

וְהַעֲבַרְתָּ שׁוֹפַר תְּרוּעָה
בַּחֹדֶשׁ הַשְּׁבִעִי בֶּעָשׂוֹר לַחֹדֶשׁ
בְּיוֹם הַכִּפֻּרִים
תַּעֲבִירוּ שׁוֹפָר בְּכָל־אַרְצְכֶם:

It is written: You shall sound a blasting shofar, t'ruah,
* in the seventh month on the tenth of the month.*
It is a Day of Atonement.
You shall sound a shofar throughout your land.
                                        —Leviticus 25:9

Why shofar t'ruah, *a blasting shofar?*
A shofar that smashes chains, breaks the power over
* all slaves.*
                                        —Zohar, Parashat Emor, 92b

T'kiah: *Listen*

THE SHOFAR HAS FOUR SOUNDS: *T'kiah* is the first, with its loud and haunting sound calling us to attention.

> *You have forgotten the truth.*
> *You have been immersed in daily life.*
> *Look into your souls and mend your ways.*
> — *Mishneh Torah*, Laws of Repentance 3:4

We think we are ready. The table is set, and the food is prepared. We bought a new outfit and fitted the children with shiny new shoes and sweet clothes. We think we are ready. We find parking in the synagogue lot or settle into the couch to watch and listen. It is the beginning of the holiday. We think we are prepared.

But we are not. As we get comfortable, we realize that we are not inspired. We are distracted by many things—seeing friends, thinking of things we need to do, remembering holidays from days long past, and longing for people who are no longer with us.

Or maybe we are simply distant, vaguely aware of what we are called to do. At work, listening to the game, going about our daily routine, oblivious or simply not interested. And if we are ready, we are ready to be bored, or maybe alienated, or maybe lost, or maybe just sleepy.

Wake up and simply listen, says our tradition. No more than that. Just listen to the eerie sound, a sound that harkens back to an ancient story and a different time. A time when Abraham thought he was obeying God and climbed a mountain to sacrifice his beloved son Isaac. That time when God's angel called him twice by name, "Abraham, Abraham." And he answered, "*Hineini.* I am here." I, too, am here. I am ready.

Abraham's ram was caught in the thicket, struggling to be free. And I sometimes feel caught in a thicket, tangled by my mediocrity, trapped by the mundane, snared by the inattention to important things, invisible things like love and forgiveness. Unable to be swept away by awe and loveliness. Caught like the ram who, when released, was sacrificed so that Isaac may live and therefore we may come into being. Freed and sacrificed so that a sound could come forth and wail through the centuries. The grand horn of the ram, the shofar, sometimes beckons the people to war or to a sacred convocation, proclaiming freedom. The shofar blasts that ancient sound on this Rosh HaShanah and commands us to awaken from the sleepy state of indifference. Awaken. Rise. Transcend. Shake and shiver the complacency from our hearts. We are majestic, proclaims the first blast. *T'kiah!* Return from the ways that lead us astray.

Return to majestic living.

Sh'varim: *Sigh*

THE SHOFAR HAS FOUR SOUNDS. The second one is *sh'varim*. Three sounds like crying, broken.

> *One sage says broken sighs, moaning. Another says wailing.*
> —Babylonian Talmud, *Rosh HaShanah* 33b

"Do you believe in calling?" she asked in a room of a thousand rabbis. I looked at her and around the great ballroom and said, "Yes," in a whisper, because others were talking of great and important things.

We speak so much of great and important things. But the heart burns with fear and worry that nothing matters and that there is little meaning to this one life we seem to have. We live within the confusing swirls of daily living.

We are called forth, born into this world within a circumstance. With parents who love us or not. With fragrant simmering pots of nourishment, overflowing and with a double portion of daily bread. Or not. We are called within a world of lack and want and squalor. We are called into this world safe or in danger, embraced or beaten. Lonely or in the company of great teachers. Or not.

"*Aychah,*" cries the prophet of Lamentations.
"How is this all possible?" he says. "What's it all for?"

"*Ayekah?*" answers the God of Adam.
"How can you hide? Where are you?"

Eich? How? Where? "I am here," we answer. "Hidden."
We search to know and seek to be known.

I am here, now, at this moment, called forth from an eternal rhythm. Beckoned to emerge from the shadows of our hiding places. To breathe, to live within the magnificence of possibility. My heart beats with a whisper—constant, consistent, never silent. And yours.

Listening to the crying tones of the shofar blast, I hear pain and notice tears. I moan and wail. I hide from my essential self, from my callings. And I know that what is broken is not lost. It is just broken, waiting for repair.

For I am called to live gently or called to live hard . . . but to live and to bring forth something good and abiding.

I carry the brilliance of ancient stardust in my bones.

And you do, as well.

T'ruah: *A Sad and Joyful Blast*

THE SHOFAR HAS FOUR SOUNDS: *T'ruah* is the third sound. It is a paradox, a broken call to joy.

> *Speak to the Israelite people thus: In the seventh month,*
> *on the first day of the month, you shall observe complete*
> *rest, a sacred occasion commemorated with* t'ruah, *with*
> *loud blasts.*
> —Leviticus 23:24

This is the call. This paradoxical sound—sharp, pounding, until joy can burst forth. Nine short blasts like the cracking of the heart that is crusty and callous. Or simply so deeply asleep that it cannot be easily roused.

T'ruah. A broken heart is an open heart, compassionate. *T'ruah.* A bruised heart is a soft heart, vulnerable. *T'ruah.* An aroused heart seeks joy, seeks to be touched by beauty, by love. *T'ruah.* A humble heart feels the rhythm, the beat, the vibration, the gentle hum of holiness.

T'ruah. Sound the shofar and assemble the people for this sacred occasion. A day of shofar song. Sing, sing to the Holy One, says the Psalmist. For the sacred melody reigns supreme. The shofar shall arouse the heart of all who hear the *t'ruah.* It is a broken sound.

Sing, sing—nine short, pounding blasts proclaiming freedom. For we have been enslaved. Slaves to our assumptions, slaves to our negativity. Slaves to what others think, or say, or demand. Slaves to our sadness. Slaves to a world that endeavors to darken our light. Happy are we who hear the broken sound of *t'ruah*; we yearn to dwell in the light of a Holy Presence.

Let this be our call: The paradoxical sound of a breaking heart bursting forth with joy. Nine short blasts like the cracking of the heart that is crusty and callous. Or so deeply asleep that it cannot be easily roused. A sound that reminds us that the human heart has infinite capacities. We can hold pain and we can hold joy at the same time. The pain does not diminish the joy, and the joy does not diminish the pain. We hold both our disappointments and the unabandoned hope that we can do better.

This is the paradox of our humanity:
Only through humility can we know greatness.
We are both empty and overflowing with possibility.
Life is at once broken and whole.

It sometimes happens
that the spirit falls into a depression,
and the person cannot find contentment
because of an awareness of their misdeeds.
Let them raise their thoughts to higher realms.
Happy is the people that know the sound of the shofar, O God,
they walk in the light of Your presence (Psalm 89:16).

—Rabbi Abraham Isaac Kook

T'kiah G'dolah: *Sustained Anticipation*

THE SHOFAR HAS FOUR SOUNDS: *T'kiah g'dolah* is the last sound. It is the sound of sustained anticipation.

The shofar blower ascends the bimah. We rise. The room is already buzzing, waiting, anticipating. The rabbi softly chants *t'kiah g'dolah*. The shofar blower stands solid and firm on the bimah. Takes a long breath and then a short breath. Lips pursed against the ram's horn, a sound enters the room. Clear, steady blast. And it sounds, and it wails, and it sings, and we squirm in our seats, nervous, anxious, listening, waiting.

This is sustained anticipation.
A collective pause, a long moment between who we were and who we aspire to be.

We tarry on this journey,
looking for the entrance to a new way. We repent, reconsider, reform, return.

We are suspended in the hope,
straddling the air like a ballerina's leap hoping to land like a wisp of beauty with a deeper love for others and even deeper love for ourselves. Delicately reaching toward things divine.

We linger in the expansive field of wonder,
enlightened by the beauty of the day's end, the closing of the gates of atonement. Envisioning. Imagining. Conceiving of what life could be like with less fear and more kindness. We long for a safe return home.

We persist—indeed pursue—deep and difficult contemplation. Alas, our flawed nature is an ever swirling of light and darkness. And though we are exhausted, we do not relent.

Forgive me, we say. I shall forgive you, we say.

And as the sound of the shofar thins, as the long blast nears its triumph end, I offer love for myself and my place in a world of holiness, goodness, and beauty. And all that is left for me to say is amen. Amen.

THE TEN DAYS OF REPENTANCE

The Broken Heart
The Injured Spirit

How great is my inner struggle,
My heart is filled with inner longing,
I crave that divine delight
Spread through my being.
                    —Rabbi Abraham Isaac Kook

My Life Is Real

THE SADNESS, the joy, the determination.

The lack of energy I feel some days,
and the commitment I feel the next day
not to give into lethargy.

The daily walks, the meals, the music.
The news reports that seep into my fears, palpable,
like the feel of desperation.

The prayers for healing and wholeness
for our world, our work, our families, our loves.

The poem that discovered me,
the hope.

Hope.

This is my
life.
It is real.

Let me enter into these Days of Holiness
grounded and uplifted,
confused and uncertain,
scared and sacred,
raw and real.

Lev Nishbar V'nidkeh:
A Broken and Humbled Heart

זִבְחֵי אֱלֹהִים רוּחַ נִשְׁבָּרָה לֵב־נִשְׁבָּר וְנִדְכֶּה אֱלֹהִים לֹא תִבְזֶה:

May my spirit, gentle and aware, be my offering
to the Holy One.
May my humbled and broken heart be my offering.
—Based on Psalm 51:19

DARKNESS COVERS THE GLORY of the moon's reflection,
only a sliver illuminates the sky.

Venus rises as a singular point of light, her name is Noga,
she is the star of love, she is the morning star,
she rises like the radiant splendor of righteousness.

I watch quietly, still.
And then, the Beloved calls out, saying:
Do not be afraid of your brokenness.
A broken heart is an open heart.
Love to the depths of your soul.

This is the season of return.

I listen lonely, alone.
And then the Beloved calls again, saying:
Do not be afraid of your power to shine,
radiant with splendor.
Love is the power that heals.

This is the season of return.

May my spirit, gentle and aware, be my offering to
the Holy One.
May my humbled and broken heart be my offering.
May this be the season of return.

Bewilderment

IN THE HOVERING WONDER of the night
I feel Your presence.

I have been lost as of late.
Floating, fluctuating between here and nowhere,
soul drifting, ungrounded, bewildered.

It is dark tonight, and the shadows are pervasive, and so
are the sounds of cars carelessly racing home from reckless
revelry, and sirens echoing off buildings of stone trying to
apprehend or to save, and felines wailing and moaning,
catting around the alleyways.

The noise endeavors to disrupt the quiet that will help me,
find me, find myself.
The world has its way.

But tonight, somehow, I am not distracted
nor dissuaded.

I am hovering in the wonderment of night, this night,
and despite the commotion and confusion
there is a gentle, persuasive presence drawing me near,
saying:

I know you are bewildered, but you must linger here a while longer;
as sure as the night is dark you are held in mercy and love.

And so, persuaded,
I wait.

Divine Discontent

"How do you see God?" asked my spiritual director. On the floor were one hundred magazine clippings. I picked the image of a single drop of water falling into a calm blue body of water, for what is God if not lucid, cool, peace?

Then she asked, "How does God see you?" Immediately I reached for the picture of two rams, strong males fighting, heads down, frozen on the page, in conflict, horns clashing.

I was born into a life of divine discontent.

Divine discontent is a persistent state of searching for something else, something more. A battle against complacency and boredom, routine and constancy. A sort of restlessness that sabotages all attempts to live a mundane, ordinary life. A fierce devotion to the extraordinary. And I have always had an unstoppable longing to understand the ineffable.

It is the call to rise out of the habit that has become our life. It is the call to rise out of complacency that keeps us set in our ways. It begs us not to settle down before our time.

Let these days be the days of divine discontent.

Let us unsettle ourselves. Allow a hairline fracture in the bone of your complacency. This is divine discontent—God's uncomfortable call to meaning, an internal restlessness like an itch in our souls that tells us that there is more to life, that there are great things to do, that there is more to learn and understand.

Zero Visibility

ONCE—more than once—I have been terrified when flying through turbulence. And once—more than once—I've said my prayers while flying through zero visibility.

It was a small aircraft, a commuter jet. I was flying to upstate New York. We probably shouldn't have taken off, but the pilot saw a small break in the fierce snowstorm. Maybe he wanted to get home. It was a Friday. Once in the air, we were stuck. The storm stretched up and down the Eastern Seaboard, and there was nowhere to go—not up, not down, not back, not forward. So we circled for an hour, and I kept wondering how much fuel was needed to ride out a storm that was fierce, large, bigger than life itself. With the subtle rocking of the airplane, my mind vacillated between two states: awareness and blankness. I would be acutely aware of everything, every noise, every motion, every expression on the flight attendant's face, every turn of the plane no matter how slight. And then I would be blank, oddly calm, and lulled into a trance by the soft hum of the engine and the blinking lights on the plane's wing illuminating the rage of the snow.

I preferred the blank state. Here, there was no fear, no thoughts, just a hum of perpetual motion and blinking red lights attempting to defy whiteout. Time passed. The storm worsened, the circle continued, no one talked—not the pilot, not the flight attendant, not the passengers. We just waited. I looked out my window and saw nothing but white on white. White snow speeding past a background of white snow. I thought to myself, *So this is what zero visibility looks like.*

Zero visibility looks like death. Or life. It is quiet, white, soft, opaque, beautiful, and terrible.

It's like that sometimes.

We can't seem to see anything at all, only the blankness of our circumstances. We get stuck in a loop, suspended above the world, far from solid ground, blinded by habit, coasting on fumes.

Daily, we choose a thousand tiny choices. We can circle endlessly, choosing to live in the present or to live in the past. Eventually, we forgive because the alternative is no longer an option. We forgive because to coast through a storm, without the ability to see beyond the pain of the moment, becomes too precarious, an impossible way to live.

Hope

LET THE CENTURIES teach me this:
From exile to exile to exile, do not succumb.
Mourn, but do not despair.
In the face of disaster, trauma, and pain, do not lose hope.
Believe in a time when it will be better.
Hope is carried on ancient particles of light.
It is the legacy of our people.

Determination, mental toughness, spiritual fortitude,
and emotional tenacity
echo from the centuries like the vibrations of a
tuning fork keeping us on key.

I practice.

Unfolding

וַאֲנִי תְפִלָּתִי־לְךָ יְהֹוָה עֵת רָצוֹן
אֱלֹהִים בְּרָב־חַסְדֶּךָ עֲנֵנִי בֶּאֱמֶת יִשְׁעֶךָ:

My life becomes a prayer to You, Holy One of Blessing,
the moment I am willing.
Answer me, O God, in grace and truth.

—Psalm 69:14

I NEED THESE DAYS to test my will, my willingness
to re-form, to transform. There is so much work

to be done

to make my life a prayer, a supplication, an utterance
of gratitude,
a living devotional.

I reach for You, Beloved.
Forgive me my trespasses. At this moment, I am willing.

Let my life be a prayer of grace and truth if You will.
I reach for You, Beloved.

I am in formation.
Unfolding.

What Is, Is

I'VE ALWAYS HATED the phrase *It is what it is*.

Sometimes, I hear a shrug in the tone of voice, a resignation: *It is what it is*. I don't believe we should resign or give up the fight or the effort or the commitment or the journey to shine, to live to the fullest. Sometimes I hear cynicism in the tone, a passive-aggressive slap, sarcasm: *Well! It is what it is*. Then there are the times that I hear a quiet sigh of desperation, a retreat into a sadness, we shrug our shoulders: *It is what it is*. Let's retire that phrase. It is a spiritual travesty, a psychological roadblock, unsupportive communication, and an act of aggression toward all that is good and beautiful in this world.

Rather, let us say, *What is, is*.
A simple change of syntax could begin a revolution in attitude, perspective, and emotional well-being. *What is, is*.
Life is a swirl of moments, some hard, some glorious. Some moments are tragic, and some are surprising bursts of wonder. It is our obligation to act, take responsibility, aspire to greatness, improve all that we can. But then we eventually reach the border, a boundary between what is in our power and what simply is not. And at that point we must decide to embark on a crossing. We leave the land of control and enter into the land of acceptance. What is, is.

I know this to be true: Just past our abilities lives a great mystery that ebbs and flows beyond the land of our comprehension. I call this living on the seam—we do what we can and release the rest. We release resistance, judgment, and the illusion of control. And then, our moments, the varied and crazy mix of realities and emotions, become softer.
Just a little south of my window live two hawks. Daily, I watch

them fly in a dance, circles of grace, wind, light, majesty. They have not left me. When I am feeling powerful, there they are. When I am feeling powerless, there they are. They draw my heart and soul toward the sky. Every day, I see the heavens as the backdrop to their constancy.

I don't know what will be. But what is, is.

The Things We Say to Ourselves

יְהִיוּ לְרָצוֹן אִמְרֵי־פִי
וְהֶגְיוֹן לִבִּי לְפָנֶיךָ
יְהֹוָה צוּרִי וְגֹאֲלִי:

May the words of my mouth
and the meditations of my heart
be acceptable to You,
O God, my Rock and my Redeemer.

—Psalm 19:15

THE WAVES of the Pacific Ocean call to me with gentle fury. I am distracted for a bit and the murmur of my inner voice sounds like waves crashing upon eternity. It is a cloudy day. The seagulls also call. I love these sounds that draw me out of my internal narrative. What we say in solitude can be so unkind. The way we beat and batter ourselves with self-doubt and deprecation, the way we blame and shame, the way of the persistent humdrum of our undisciplined minds that tells us that *we can't* and *we shouldn't* and *how dare we*. And perhaps to add insult to the injuries we carry, we are often unaware of this internal monologue and the constant chatter. It is the white noise of disdain. To change the negative narrative, we first need to become aware of what we say to ourselves when no one is listening.

So, this morning, this cloudy and misty morning, I am grateful for the rumble of the waves asking me to discover a kinder voice and to consider and reconsider my place in the world, my actions and behaviors, my tendencies, and my habits. The words I use to describe myself and the stories that I have told over and over keep me stuck in beliefs that no longer serve me. In this self-awakening, this self-reckoning, I have learned to handle negative thoughts gently but firmly. *Thank you*, I say. *You have served me in the past, but you serve me longer. I release you.*

One unkind thought at a time.
Release them to the wind, to the waves, to the mist.
And then replace them with kindness.

What would you say if you were to tell your story as a blessing rather than a curse? If you would whisper sweet nothings of love to your wounded spirit, what would they be? If you would sit upon the mountain's edge and listen to waves as old as time, would you remember that you are connected to a transcendent power?

Walk gently upon this earth. Lift your eyes and let go of the tension in your jaw. Straighten your burdened shoulders with determination. We need resolve to change, to live in kindness.

And as the holy day beckons, I will go to be among the myriads of people who search for sanctuary within the company of community. Still, I know that it is the inner narrative that needs to shift if I am to shift.

Yom Kippur

Returning Home
Forgiveness and Repentance

Three gifts—three faculties—are given to us to
  draw us toward God.
Our conscience knows right and wrong.
Our heart feels love.
Our soul makes us susceptible to wonder and awe.
                              —Rabbi Jonathan Wittenberg

Soft and Sharp Edges

MY FORGIVENESS has soft edges,
it is compassion,
it is self-care
and spiritual survival.

And sharp edges.
I feel the brutality of my circumstances.
And yours?

We will emerge from this better.

Kol Nidrei

אוֹר זָרֻעַ לַצַּדִּיק וּלְיִשְׁרֵי־לֵב שִׂמְחָה:

Light is sown for the righteous,
radiance and joy for the pure of heart.

—Psalm 97:11

With one voice, assembled Sages past and present declare:
All may pray as one on this night of repentance;
Let none be excluded from our community of prayer.

—*Mishkan HaNefesh: Machzor for the Days of Awe; Yom Kippur*

IN THE EVENING, with darkness outside and a murmur of anticipation inside, we gather. It is *Kol Nidrei* and we have left our family meals dressed beautifully—perhaps in the traditional white, perhaps in something new, perhaps with a tallit, perhaps with a piece of our mother's jewelry. We come with our aging parents, and we are wondering if this will be their last *Kol Nidrei*. We come with squirming children who sense that something special is happening. We come alone, maybe lonely, not sure if we belong, or maybe glad for a private moment amidst the crowd of others. We arrive and the flowers are white, and the Torah mantles are white and the silver polished, and the choir is humming, and the clergy—humble, anxious, ready—have the air of serene heaviness.

We gather—open with expectation, spiritually vulnerable, or maybe defensive. We hope to be moved, carried away, changed. Cracked open.

Please rise, and we see the leaders of our community aging, noting the passage of time, mortality, as they hold the heavy Scrolls of Mystery and Story and History and Divine Command and Hope and Moral Imperative. We stand for a very long time. Shifting in our place. Listening as if in a timeless trance to the hypnotic repetition of sounds, which are at once ancient, distant, familiar, traditional, personal, and penetrating.

Shifting, watching, listening, spacing out to a different space. The cadence, alliteration, assonance, repetition, metaphor, and symbol become the wordless meaning. The Aramaic words are foreign, and the translation is confusing. The text is legal rhetoric whose origin and precise meaning and purpose are lost to history. *Kol Nidrei* proclaims that all our vows are now annulled:

> *All vows—resolves and commitments, vows of abstinence and terms of obligation, sworn promises and oaths of dedication—that we promise and swear to God and take upon ourselves from this Day of Atonement until next Day of Atonement, may it find us well: we regret them and for all of them we repent. Let all of them be discarded and forgiven, abolished and undone; they are not valid and they are not binding.*

But knowingly or unknowingly we are resolved to the imperfections of the status quo. We vow, bonded by habit and inertia, to be unmoved. We cannot escape the reality of our humanity, which is flawed. We change, if we change at all, ever so slowly. Afraid of the hard and painful work it takes to be more self-aware of the promises we have made to the family way, to the generational hurt and trauma, to the habit of limping as if there is a forever pebble in our shoe that slows us down. We are rooted in our unkind, unjust ways.

And the music begins, and the cantor stands strong. Cadence, alliteration, assonance, repetition, metaphor, and symbol become more primary than the denotative or connotative meaning of the text. The imagery, symbolism, and metaphor lay not in the words but rather in the pageantry. We become the poem, participating in a symbolic moment and anticipating something grand.

The power of poetry lies not in the expression of ideas but rather in the images, sounds, and associations. Meaning is found in a flash of a moment rather than explicative thought. The white garb becomes a metaphor for purity; the new clothes become a metaphor for a new beginning. The Torah scrolls represent spirals of meaning, the commanding voice of history and morality, of story and ethics, of behavior and belief. We hear the sounds of *Kol Nidrei*, feel the weight of the moment, and see the possibilities of a life where goodness is common and the highest expression of ourselves prevails. We are the pageantry. We are the poem. This is a moment of transcendence.

The Story Is Told: Repentance Is Healing

RABBI CHAMA BAR CHANINA said:
Great is repentance,
for it brings healing to the world.

As it is written:
I will heal them as they return,
I will love them freely.

Repentance is healing.
> —*Based on Babylonian Talmud,* Yoma 86a

A New Iteration

WE WERE OUT FOR BREAKFAST at a café on Kibbutz Dafna in the Upper Galilee. It was a quaint, earthy place, nestled in among trees, not far from one of the tributaries of the Jordan River. Breakfast comes with eggs made to order, freshly squeezed orange juice or lemonade, coffee, latte, espresso filtered or brewed, an array of soft and hard cheeses, freshly made breads, and locally grown vegetable salad, cut small and dressed with lemon and olive oil. We ate. And as we love to do, we became thoughtful, philosophical about our lives.

There's no cure for being me, my daughter said to me as we talked about life, destiny, pain, and soul. We giggled. So very true. And actually, we wouldn't have it any other way, we acknowledged. We are all scrapped and scratched. We are all a bit bumpy and lumpy in places. We are all in need of repair.

Alas, perfection is not a condition of humanity. What then? If we cannot realistically expect a cure or real change, then what is this path we are on? With every step, I take me with me.

Lately I've been saying that I am working to find the next iteration of me. This language suits me better. Whatever living has embedded itself into our psyche, into the spirit, it is there to stay. There are no exorcisms for the parts we don't like. The process is not one of change where the hurt and imperfections vanish and no longer matter. They matter. And always will. We strive to recognize the hurt, understand the imperfections, embrace the inadequacies, and then we can use them as motivation for deeper capacities. May we use our pain for empathy, compassion, understanding, forgiveness.

Changing

GOD, SCATTER all the pieces of my life,
like the wind against these autumn leaves.

I shall gather and collect the brittle beauty
and await the flowering of change.

Asked, Called, Commanded

WE ARE BEING ASKED.

Asked to apologize, sometimes
more than once.
To say I'm sorry.
Really I am.

And we are being called.

Called to step out of hiding,
out of the shadows,
and look honestly and deeply
to see if our life's purpose aligns with who we are.

There is gold dust in our souls; there are nuggets and gems
that wait to be mined and polished. There is buried treasure
waiting to adorn our lives, to add glint to the world.

We are being called.

Called out of oblivion into meaning.
Called to live a glorious life of consequence.
We are strong, and wise, and simple,
and we are called to do more.

We are healers, we are warriors, we are faithful companions
of the lost soul.
We owe so much to the world. How gracious are we in
donating our beauty?

But first, we are being commanded.

To make amends,
sometimes more than once.
To say forgive me.
Please forgive me.

The Mishnah states: To those who say, "I will sin and
repent, I will sin and repent,"
Yom Kippur offers no atonement.
For sins against God, Yom Kippur offers atonement.
For sins against another, Yom Kippur offers
no atonement
until you seek reconciliation with the one you
have wronged.
                    —*Mishnah Yoma* 8:9

I Am the Builder and You Are the Landscape

I AM BUILDING MY LIFE. I am the architect and the contractor. And the ditch digger, digging deep so that I may have a strong foundation. I get down on my knees to pray, to lay the floor. I need support as I wander from room to room.

I have built the attic for my sorrows, a kitchen to gather and share wisdom, a sitting room to sit and read and laugh and invite.

I have built many rooms to dwell in privacy, unseen, naked, sleeping, quiet, and desperate. Windows and doors of course. There's always a way out. There's always a way in.

And like my relationships, the landscape is varied.

The
delicate buttercups blanket the worn lawns of Maryland. When held under your chin, reflect a yellow light. The children of Maryland say that is proof that someone loves you.

Somebody loves you.

The
tall grasses of Illinois that are best seen from a distance, looking light like feathers as the wind has its way. But up close, they are too dense to walk among.

And some people are beautiful from a distance.

The
aspens of the West, sturdy, vibrating. They seem so unyielding, yet they are in constant motion.

You know who they are.

The
bluebonnets of Texas grow by the side of the road. They may
not be touched, as mandated by the laws of Texas.

Leave them be, wild and lovely.

And the garden variety of perennials and annuals. Because
some people come and go and some stay. And the maple on
my lawn and the lilacs and roses. And the dandelions and
clover. Flowers and weeds. You know who they are as well.

I build my home and my relationships upon your landscape.
My inner life is so varied and complicated.

Forgiveness

I ASK FOR FORGIVENESS,
to be better, to do better, to expand my capacity.

To reflect light upon the dark corners of my soul,
upon the dark world that waits to be redeemed.

Hold me in mercy, dear God. Hold me with grace
as my light is revealed during these Days of Awe.

הֲלוֹא אִם־תֵּיטִיב שְׂאֵת
וְאִם לֹא תֵיטִיב לַפֶּתַח חַטָּאת רֹבֵץ
וְאֵלֶיךָ תְּשׁוּקָתוֹ וְאַתָּה תִּמְשָׁל־בּוֹ:

Surely, if you do right,
you are uplifted, exalted.

But if you do not do right,
sin couches at the door;

Its urge is toward you,
yet you can be its master.

—Genesis 4:7

Drifting Home

I AM DRIFTING, unmoored from what has anchored me. Adrift. Whispering wind. Quiet waters. The tide will bring me home. I understand that if I am to find my way home, it is with the currents and the tides. It is with the waves and the winds. It is with the pull of the moon, a reflective luminary. I need this moment. I am at peace. At one. This is my atonement. To give over control, pull up the anchor and in the forgiving waters, drift, saying, I am sorry. I am sorry that I did not say I love you enough. I did not embrace you enough. I am sorry.

Quiet waters, whispering wind take me home.

Seven Practices Toward Awakening

Awake, awake you sleepers from your sleep; examine
your deeds, return in repentance, remember your
Creator; those of you who forget the truth and go astray
the whole year in vanity and emptiness that neither
profits nor saves, look to your souls.

—Maimonides, *Mishneh Torah*, Laws of Repentance 3:4

AWAKE

Slowly, for awakening takes time. I open my eyes and see that there can be a different way of living your life. I stretch my arms wide open and then fold them into a loving embrace. I lift my head toward the horizon of possibility, unknown but possible. I straighten my back to bear the burden of another. Awake. Am I sleeping through the chance to be grand, to do good, to live a holy, considered life?

Awake slowly. Settle down. Settle in. Stay a while.

Awake you sleepers from your sleep
This is the secret of the world. It always hums and whistles a sacred tune. But I live with noise, canceling out the melody. The cars, the shouting, the busy, the whining, and the over-active way of being are deafening and lull the sacred hearing into a resting sleep, waiting to awaken.

Settle down. Settle in. Stay a while.

Return in repentance
Return means to turn. Stale, stuck, sedentary, I need only to turn around. When I am racing, rushing, oblivious, turn around. When I am wrong, uncaring, filled with self-interest, I turn around. When I am no-where, I must turn around. And be still. Now-here. Returning, turning around,

turning inward, turning back to the Source of mercy and for-giveness and kindness. It takes time.

Settle down. Settle in. Stay a while.

Remember your Creator
Return also means retune. Tune into the sacred hum. Beyond the noise is quiet. Beyond the quiet is song. Linger there because, beyond the song, you will find your purpose. Now I remember the Source of all that is truly good and truly mighty. I remember that my power is so small—so small that it is liberating.

Retuning, remembering, is a practice of time. It is a differ-ent way of using time. Retune. I am trying to remember the divine purpose of my life.

Settle down. Settle in. Stay a while.

Those of you who forget the truth and go astray the whole year in vanity and emptiness that neither profits nor saves
We have forgotten. We have given away the soulful knowing of who we are, of why we are, of where we are. We attach our-selves to the vanities of this world—money, prestige, status, and the opinions of others. And they have so many opinions. We can be of this world and enjoy the things of life. We can take pleasure from wealth and reputation. But attachment to those things leads to suffering. In the world of accumu-lation and self-importance, there is never enough. Let our endeavors and strivings be brought into balance. For today we confront our mortality. And here is the truth: We are but dust and ashes. And also, a little lower than the angels. We live our life in the in-between of those two truths. Endeavor with humility. Let your strivings be attached for a holy pur-pose. This takes time to understand.

Settle down. Settle in. Stay a while.

Look to your souls

Let us live from the inside out. Deep within the quiet murmurings of our soul, there is much wisdom. God whispers of sweet nothings. We know so much if we can only learn to listen. To discern meaning from the spirit that is restless, sometimes breathless, trying to get our attention. We have been called to attention. Awaken the spirit, set aside the daily discourse, and enter into another conversation. A conversation with your soul-work that banishes a secret sense of alienation. Connecting, returning to the beautiful person we were born to be. Busy with sparkle and splendor and true matters of consequence.

Settle down. Settle in. Stay a while.

The Paradox

Let us not be so stiff-necked as to say we have not
sinned, for surely, we have sinned.

WE ARE FLAWED. And we are beautiful.
We are kind. And we are unkind.
Sometimes we do justly, love mercy,
   and walk softly with God.
Sometimes we simply behave badly.

We live within a paradox that toggles between right and wrong. This is the paradox of the human condition.

We believe in the goodness of Creation and the goodness of our spirit. But we are undeniably flawed. Fundamental to our very nature, manifested in our character, made painfully evident in our daily struggle, we choose to behave badly. We are so often overcome by the inclination to give in to our fears, greed, gossip, meanness, and indifference. We are egotistical and self-centered. We have sinned.

We translate *cheit* as "sin," but faithful to the Hebrew, it would be better rendered as "missing the mark." Imagine a master archer, distracted—for a moment, her eye looks away and she lets the arrow fly from the bow. Most likely, she misses the mark, which is the center of the target. So is *cheit*—distracted, we go astray. These days are about focus, aim, and commitment to the moral art of good.

For we *are* good. This is our core belief. We are foundationally good. We recount our origin story from the very creation of our world and of humankind and see the word "good" proclaimed after each creative act (and on the third day, when sea and dry land and trees and seed-bearing plants are created, it is said twice).

Daily, waking from the nighttime wandering of our dreams and slumber, whether restless or sound, we recite, *I am grateful to You, O God, who has returned my spirit to me with* chemlah, *divine mercy.* And we continue: *God, the soul You have given me is pure.*

Just as the dawn begins to banish the darkness of the night, we affirm that the light of a new day is like the light of Creation, good in its very essence, and it mingles with gratitude, mercy, and purity. They are qualities and inclinations that are as real as the stardust of Creation. This is our daily affirmation. So when we stray, when we miss the mark of goodness, we refocus, take better aim, return to a path that is our inheritance, and try to incline our ways to goodness.

According to our origin story, as we read in the first verses of the Book of Genesis, the world is created with the word *bara*—a unique creation that bursts forth with light from a primordial nothingness. But, as our story continues, humans are formed with a different word, *yatzar*, from the dust of the earth and animated by God with the breath of life we call the soul.

וַיִּיצֶר יְהֹוָה אֱלֹהִים אֶת־הָאָדָם עָפָר מִן־הָאֲדָמָה
וַיִּפַּח בְּאַפָּיו נִשְׁמַת חַיִּים
וַיְהִי הָאָדָם לְנֶפֶשׁ חַיָּה:

God formed [vayitzer] *the human from the dust of the earth,*
blowing into his nostrils the breath of life:
the human became a living being.

—Genesis 2:7

That word *yatzar* describes not only our physical formation but also the tendencies and inclinations of our moral and ethical formation. From that very first moment, we are destined to oscillate between two types of *yatzar* formations. One we call *yetzer tov*, "the inclination to good"—goodness true to our creation with purity and mercy. And the other *yetzer hara*, "the inclination to bad"—missing the mark of goodness, purity of soul, and divine mercy. Our inclinations oscillate between good and bad, between compassion and indifference, between kindness and anger. Sometimes we behave according to our true nature, and sometimes we miss the mark. That is why we are here now. To find our true nature. To correct our ways. Refocus, aim, center.

Confession

אֲנִי יְשֵׁנָה וְלִבִּי עֵר

קוֹל דּוֹדִי דוֹפֵק

פִּתְחִי־לִי.

I am asleep, but my heart is awakened.
My Beloved knocks upon the gate.
Open.

— Song of Songs 5:2

LOST,
trying to find a clearing
in the thicket,
I lay down
my machete
and sat at the edge,
lingering a long while.

As the sun began to set
and the shadows darkened
questions arose and so I asked:

When did I become hesitant,
afraid of failure, and the journey's joy turned foreboding?
And when did I become scared, unclear? Afraid of
   my mortality?

I was once fearless and brave.

A deep sleep fell upon me, until, quite unexpectedly,
in the middle of the night, I heard a song:

Awake, O north wind! Come, O south wind!
This tangled thicket is but an overgrown garden,
awaiting my confession.

And then in the wind of the early dawn, a faint melody—

I was asleep, but my heart is awake. Listen!
The sound of my Beloved is knocking:
"Open to me, my sister, my darling, my dove,
    my innocent one.
My head is drenched with dew, my hair with the
    dampness of the night."

The Beloved was hidden, gone from me,
and now beckons like the wind of the receding night.
Open, open the locked gate.
Open.

And I lay weeping, breathless,
confessing my inadequacies,
my hardened fearful heart,
my hesitation to love fully,
to act with patience,
to live with abiding kindness.

And with each confession, an opening.
A clearing
appeared
in the thicket.
And with each
fragile step,
my fears
began to lift like the morning dew.

Confessing.

Draw Us Near

הֲשִׁיבֵנוּ, וְנָשׁוּבָה.
Hashiveinu, v'nashuvah.
Draw us near, and we shall return.
—Lamentations 5:21

THE FOG blurred my vision. I could not see the other side of the river, no matter how much I shifted and squinted. It was simply obscured. And oddly beautiful. And madly inviting. You see, it is not always clear how to return home, but the longing to return is oh so clear. It is the pull toward better, safer, kinder living. It is the tug toward a familiar yet distant shore where life is a little less complicated. It is that need to straighten things out a bit and to remember the why and wherefore of living.

But on this day, I couldn't see my way back. You see, the fog obscured my way. So I waited a long while. And on that day and the days that followed—and the years too—I tarried in my desire of return. And while waiting for the fog to lift, I learned so much about the why and wherefore of my life. I learned that when a lost soul has the tenacity to linger in the desire for betterment, that too is a kind of revelation.

How powerful is our Hebrew word for repentance, *t'shu-vah*? In English, the word implies a theology of contrition and sometimes shame, a spiritual conversion from a state of sin to one of righteousness. But in Hebrew, the word *t'shuvah* simply means "return." And in another form, the Hebrew root can mean "to sit, to settle, to settle down, to settle in." What a linguistic paradox! Sometimes *t'shuvah* is to spiritually move, to take a journey, a return home. And sometimes it is a spiritual settling down, staying put. It has taken me years to reach this point, merely sitting by the river, sometimes in a fog for a very long time. We learn that, too, can deepen, heal, and instruct the soul that seeks to return. It has for me.

Happy are those who sit still in the presence of God, and happy are those who find strength in God, directing their hearts and minds to the byways.

Joy is found in both—the sitting and the dwelling, and in the hope of the journey, of return.

We sing, *Hashiveinu, v'nashuvah.* Yet a different dimension of the same root, but this time the word means "to reach": *Reach for us, Holy One, draw us near so that we may return.* Maybe like the lighthouse on that foggy day, it is a beacon of hope, showing us the way, tugging at us to do this life better.

We are so unkind and critical about our imperfections. My life has been a wandering of stray and return, stray and return. I have fallen so many times, tripped by the imperfections and the scars of living. But I have not, even once, strayed from my desire to be better, brighter, enlightened, more kind. And that too, that too is *t'shuvah.*

T'shuvah is in the tarry, the reach, and the return. Somedays it's all so clear. And some days not.

That too.

וַאֲנִי אָמַרְתִּי נִגְרַשְׁתִּי מִנֶּגֶד עֵינֶיךָ
אַךְ אוֹסִיף לְהַבִּיט אֶל־הֵיכַל קָדְשֶׁךָ:

I thought I was driven away
from Your presence:
Would I ever gaze again
upon Your holy Temple?
—Jonah 2:5

The Story Is Told: Look for a New Way

ONCE OUR TEACHER Rabbi Hayyim of Zans told a parable: A person had been wandering about the forest for several days, not knowing which was the way out. Suddenly they saw a person approaching. Their heart filled with joy and they thought, "Now I shall find out which is the right way!" When the two neared one another, one said to the other, "Friend, can you tell me the right way? I have been wandering in the forest for several days."

The other replied, "I do not know the way out either. For I too have been wandering about for many, many days. But *this* I can tell you: Do not take the way I have been taking, for that will lead you astray. And now let us look for a new way together."

Our teacher added, "So it is with us. One thing I can tell you: The way we have been following this far we ought to follow no further, for that way leads one astray. But now let us look for a new way, together."

—S. Y. Agnon

Sh'ma Koleinu: *Hear Me*

HEAR ME,

show me compassion with grace and care,
show me the way back to You, let me return as in
    the days of old.

Do not cast me away from Your presence,
and do not cast me away as I grow old, diminished
    of strength.

Do not forsake me, let me feel You near.

With hope, I await Your presence.

May the words of my mouth and the meditations of
    my heart be acceptable.

Repentance

Is this the right word?

Try this:

contrition
anguish
penitence
regret
remorse
acknowledgment of error
sorrow
conscience
making amends
distress
compassion

That too.

Three Sins

There are three sins that do not wait for Yom Kippur
but come before God for immediate judgment:

walking next to a shaky wall, trusting that your merit
will keep the wall from falling on you

being pompous in prayer, believing that you are so
righteous that your prayers will be answered

and asking God to judge someone else, which only
causes you, the accuser, to be judged first.
    —Based on Babylonian Talmud, *Rosh HaShanah* 16b

RABBI JUDITH Z. ABRAMS, PhD, *z"l*, was a classmate and a friend. She would drive me to school from the suburbs to Clifton, where our rabbinical seminary was. Once, I remember her darting in and out of lanes a little too fast for the morning rush. She claimed that there was a method, almost a science, to beat the rush hour slog. She learned it from her father. I don't know where her father learned it.

Brilliant, in love with Talmud, she later commented about the quote above:

> *This is my favorite piece of Gemara* [Rabbinic commentary on the Mishnah]. *In essence, it says, don't bring God's judgment upon yourself by judging another harshly or yourself leniently.*

While driving in traffic, I suppose Judy was dodging obstacles by weaving in and out of lanes. I don't know what I mean by this, I just know that I am dodging judgments all the time.

Don't judge them so harshly, I whisper.
And, I continue, *how would you be if you held yourself accountable just a bit more?*

Forgive Me

Know that each and every shepherd has his or her
*   own unique tune.*
Know that each and every blade of grass has its own
*   unique song.*
And from the songs of the grass, the tune of the
*   shepherd is created.*
How beautiful, how beautiful and fine when we
*   hear their song.*
It is very good to pray between them and to labor
*   for God with awe.*
And the song of the grass causes the heart to awaken
*   and to long.*

—Rebbe Nachman of Bratzlav

THE TALL GRASSES sing a song, said Rebbe Nachman from Bratzlav. He would go into the forest in the middle of the night to hear that sacred melody. Often sad, or even depressed, he would wander among the trees with the birds as his companions, lifting his hands toward the gazing light of the constellations. Hear me. See me. Do not forsake me, sing me a song of redemption, he would implore.

And in this moment, far from the Rebbe in time and space, I too listen for the melody of the tall grasses. I too sit in supplication, praying to be heard and forgiven. Forgive me.

> *S'lach lanu*, I pray.
> Forgive me, O God, for my complexities.
> I ask to live with simplicity,
> to love mercy, to do justly, to walk humbly.
> *M'chal lanu*, I implore.
> I want only to find the way toward forgiveness.

I ask to live simply.
To forgive, to ask for forgiveness, to accept
forgiveness.

Kaper lanu, I fervently sing.
Awaken a compassionate sensibility within us.
I ask only to live deeply.
Lift me, shake me, take me.

I strain to be the song that will carry my prayer,
that will hold my supplication.
This year, this moment, this time I shall do better.

The Story Is Told: Gossip

A CERTAIN PERSON is brought before the rabbi, having been accused of gossiping. They insist they have done no wrong. It was just an opinion, after all, and surely not their responsibility if others choose to repeat it. Still, they agree to ask for forgiveness.

The rabbi explains it isn't that simple and asks if they have a pillow. Of course, they do—they have the finest, softest down pillow in the village.

The rabbi instructs them to go fetch the pillow and climb to the top of a hill. Once there, the rabbi tells them to tear open the pillow and scatter the feathers to the wind. Standing on the hill, they release the feathers while repeating their excuses as they watch each one drift away.

The person returns to the rabbi and says, "Am I now forgiven?"

"It is not quite that easy," the rabbi says. "Go now and gather up the feathers and stuff them back into the pillow." They try, stammering and struggling, to collect the feathers but return with only a few in hand.

"What have you learned?" the rabbi asks.

"Well, I suppose my words are like the feathers. Once words are spoken, they are hard to gather up again."

—*Rabbi Levi Yitzchak of Berditchev*

What Is Said, Is Said

THE DOWN PILLOW is torn,
and its feathers scatter in the wind,
resting here and there, near and far.
Try as we might,
it is impossible to gather them.
Just as our unkind words scatter here and there
and it is impossible to repair the damage.

What Can I Say?

When Mar, son of Ravina, would conclude his prayers,
he would say this:
"My God, keep my tongue from evil and my lips from
deceitful speech" (Psalm 34:14).
—Babylonian Talmud, *B'rachot* 17a

IN OUR CONFESSIONAL prayer called *Al Cheit*, we count for-ty-four sins—a double acrostic, with two sins for each letter of the Hebrew alphabet. In some traditions, twelve of these sins relate to the things we say.

It is said:
Gossip kills three people: the gossip, the listener, and the person they are talking about.

The prophet says, *Their tongue is a sharpened arrow.*
The tongue kills like an arrow that is fired from a bow. It travels a great distance.

A person's tongue is more powerful than their sword.
A sword can kill somebody who is nearby; a tongue can cause the death of someone who is far away.

YOM KIPPUR

Return Home
Character and Moral Compass

Let us not think that repentance is only necessary
for sins such as wantonness, robbery, or theft.
We are certainly obligated to repent from these.

And we are also asked to examine the nature of our character.
To turn away from anger, hatred, envy, and frivolity.

To repent from the pursuit of money and honor,
the pursuit of gluttony, and so much more.

These sins are difficult to turn away from.
They are habits, learned behaviors, familiar ways of being.

We are attached to these traits,
so separating ourselves from them is more difficult.

It is a fundamental challenge to change the way we are
   used to being.

—Based on Maimonides, *Mishneh Torah*,
Laws of Repentance 7:3

Character

WE RESPOND to circumstances, people, and our own emotions out of habit formed over a lifetime. We are held accountable for our convictions, and the words we use, and the silences we keep. It matters when we stand up for what is right and when we sit down next to the one who cannot stand.

We are judged not only by our kindness but also by our anger.

Our crime is not only what we have stolen from a client but also from the hearts we have broken.

Not only from the houses we have robbed but also from the tender souls we have criticized.

Not only from the times we have embraced but also from the times we have not reached out.

And for all these, we atone.

For this and more, we try to learn to break those habits that tarnish the shine of the person we yearn to be. We try to release the rote reactions that lead us astray.

With humility and a genuine desire to become better, to be better, we enter into a holy space of reckoning; it is not only what we do but also who we are that defines us.

For all these things and more—atonement.

The Story Is Told: So Says the Prophet

Is IT THE FAST that I desire?
A day for people to starve their bodies?
Is it bowing of your head like a bulrush
or lying in sackcloth and ashes, that I require?

Do you call this a fast,
a day desired by the Holy One?

No, this is the fast I desire:

To release the chains of wickedness,
to untie the cords that bind the yoke.

Let the oppressed go free,
break the yoke that binds them.

Share your bread with the hungry,
invite the poor to the bounty of your table.

When you see the naked, clothe them,
do not turn away from your people.

Then your light shall burst forth like the dawn
and your healing shall quickly flower.

—Based on Isaiah 58:5–8

All My Life

ALL MY LIFE, I have sacrificed on many altars.
My life has been an offering to the greater good.
Sometimes I forget that it is deeds of love and
acts of kindness that atone for so much.

So much.

The Story Is Told: So Says the Prophet

GOD WILL ANSWER when you cry and say, "I am here."

Offer your compassion to the hungry, for they have no meal waiting at home. Then God will say, "I am here." And your light shall shine in the darkness, and your gloom shall be like the noonday.

Climb the mountain of prayer and repentance. Sit cross-legged at the pinnacle, noticing your breath, saying the words, and denying yourself an ordinary day.

Then come down from the mountaintop into the streets and put your hand on the shoulder of another. "How can I help?" you should say. "How can I ease your pain?"

—Based on Isaiah 58

A Moral Compass

עֹשֶׂה כִימָה וּכְסִיל
וְהֹפֵךְ לַבֹּקֶר צַלְמָוֶת וְיוֹם לַיְלָה הֶחְשִׁיךְ...
יְהֹוָה שְׁמוֹ:

Who made the Pleiades and Orion,
Who turns deep darkness into dawn
and darkens day into night . . .
Whose name is God.

—Amos 5:8

WANDERING in a moonless night, the desert hides its vast-ness and vistas. It is a dark depth, like the pupil of the eye of some unknown God. I struggle not to feel lost. Not to lose my sense of place. My place in this dark desert world has no discernible path, no sense of where the desert wadi ends and the steep mountain climb begins. I can't see the wild hog, lethal when it charges to protect its young. I can't see the blonde scorpion, the snake, or the red spider. I can see the majesty and the terror of night—nothing more, nothing less. And less is more in the desert, in this wilderness that finds me wandering in the dark, avoiding danger. Darkness is only bad when you go astray.

And I can hear. I hear the resounding silence. When I struggle and strain against it, it is uncomfortable and disori-enting. But if I sit still, I hear the desert song, an ancient mel-ody of dissonance and harmony. Dissonance and harmony are the foundation of all spiritual endeavors. And I endeavor.

It sings:

Stay still, stay still.

Oh, darkness be my womb and not my grave.

Dear silence, be my God, the voice of purpose
and righteousness.

And then, quite suddenly, I notice what has always been there—the constellations that twinkle and glimmer, piercing the darkness with a billion illuminations. I am not lost if only I look up. There, in the sky, as big as any reality imaginable, stands the warrior of the night, Orion. In Hebrew, his name is Kasil. His arms are extended in supplication, his feet wide, planted in the heavens with steady grace. And his warrior's belt is holding his sword while pointing to the North Star. Fight your way through this complicated life, it seems to say. Or follow the North Star and journey forth. I follow the North Star; it shows me the way.

Intentionally, inadvertently, we stumble, speak with careless disregard, and behave recklessly. We are often unkind. Maybe because we are hurt, we hurt others. Maybe because we forget how much power we have, we wield it thoughtlessly. Maybe because we are afraid, we lash out. Maybe because we are careless, we behave badly.

We blurt and fumble and become the scorpion in someone's dark night.

And though things are often unclear, as in a dark desert night, there is right and there is wrong. There is good and there is bad. Every time we wander off the path of purpose, of kindness, of goodness, of humility, of generosity, of honesty, of quiet listening, we diminish the glimmer that lights the world.

Expand the light. Lift your eyes to the heavens. Orion points to the North Star so that you may find your way.

As it is written:

A sound is heard from the desert. Find the path, a straight path in the Arava wilderness.

The Mapmaker

OFF THE COAST of eastern Asia, the mapmaker drew a boundary with heavy black paint. And then, on the other side of the line, he wrote in blue simply, *Hic sunt dracones*, "Here be dragons." The year was 1510, and the map was on a small red copper globe about 4.5 inches in diameter. In 1870 this globe was gifted to James Lenox by Richard Morris Hunt. Lenox's private collection became the foundation of the New York Public Library. Today the globe rests in the Rare Book Division of the library. It was the oldest globe known in existence until recently, when a globe drawn on an ostrich egg surfaced. It is presumed to be a few years earlier than the Lenox globe. It bears the same inscription: *Hic sunt dracones*, "here be dragons."

Nobody knows what the mapmakers meant by this, but the phrase "Here be dragons" has captured the imagination of poets and philosophers, mapmakers and rare book collectors. For years it has captured my imagination as well.

With all its ambiguity, we know that beyond the borders of integrity and kindness, of compassion and justice, dragons roam. We open the *machzor*, the book of High Holy Day prayer, and see a spiritual map that has been drawn by our tradition, by the rabbis and liturgists of yore, by our sense of divine command. The *machzor* reveals the byways and passages that lead us toward human decency and away from ethical travesty. Throughout the holy day we are warned that we must not stray from the path, and so we confess. We stand at the gate of repentance and proclaim, "*Al cheit shechatanu l'fanecha*—for the sins that we have sinned." Our recitation is rhythmic, drawing us back to stay within the boundaries. And yet there are a myriad of ways we have crossed over, traditionally forty-four—two for every letter in the Hebrew alphabet. For the sin of gossip, of slander, of envy, of falsehood, of hate, of anger, of obstinance—*al cheit shechatanu l'fanecha*.

Shuvu, shuvu—return, return to the path of righteousness, says our tradition. Return to goodness, return to faithfulness, return to love. *Shuvu, shuvu*—come back within the boundaries, the mapmaker warns. Beyond here, dragons roam.

YOM KIPPUR

Return to Love

In the morning I thought:
"Life's magic will never return,
it won't return."
Suddenly in my house, the sun
is a living thing,
And the table with its bread—
gold.
And the flower and the cups—
gold.
And the sadness?
Even there—
radiance.

                    —Zelda

An Invitation

LOVE IS NOT A FEELING, it is a practice.
And an invitation.

Forty days to think, to break open an encrusted heart, to remember sweetness and innocence, to live with hope rather than bitterness. Forty days to recognize that our bad behaviors are the antithesis of love. Forty days to wonder, to ponder what it means to practice love, to be in love, to be loved. To linger in the radical thought that the universe is held with love. Tarry in the invitation to return to love.

I am my beloved's and my beloved is mine is an affirmation, an assertion that the foundation of the spiritual universe is love. We endeavor to find one another, to fall in love, and to offer love. But there is a love beyond relationships. We believe this is a transcendent love, the deepest desire of the heart. To love, to be loved, to be beloved.

In the spiritual world, the opposite of love is fear. Our hurts and rejections constrict our expansive thinking. We believe that somehow our place in the universe is a place of scarcity where love and acceptance are withheld. We are afraid to be denied the love we so desire and so we behave badly. Bad behavior is fear-based behavior. Anger, guilt, jealousy, cruelty, gossip, betrayal are all manifestations of fear.

Whatever the question, love is the answer. We spend much time lost and deflated, scared and dismayed. Love is the answer. We lose our way, wander from the path, and lose a sense of direction. Love is the answer. We care too much, not enough, and become flat, bored, silly. Love is the answer. Love is our connection to the sublime; it awakens our capacity to see beauty, to dwell in beauty. It is a state of being that is expansive, that lives in possibility, that will not let hope die.

Spiritual love is the acute awareness that we are connected and that all is connected, allowing us to transcend our fears, our insecurities, our limited capacities. We reach beyond the smallness of self. We become large, bountiful, great. Loving.

This is the season we return to love.

Acceptance

ACCEPT THE COURSE of your life with kindness and
compassion.

No judgment.
Only love.

It twists like a sailor's knot,
it turns like an erratic wind.

It seeks the harbor,
it is lost at sea.

There are good days,
there are bad days.

It is complicated
intricate
simple.

Find yourself
maybe tired, maybe satisfied, maybe wounded,
maybe healed, maybe not.
Accepting.

This is your life's story,
sometimes lost and sometimes found,
then lost and found, and lost and found again.

Find yourself in a loving embrace
better than before, better than ever,

held tight by the gift of time

and the knowing
that life is to be honored and revered.

Certain Words

THERE ARE CERTAIN WORDS I have always loved. Mostly for their sound. Like when my eight-year-old cousin would say to his fraternal twin, "You're pathetic." I loved the sound of that word, the way his intonation would make it bounce in the middle. And then, years later, I realized I was a student of the pathetic, trying not to be pathetic, by which I meant complaining, lazy, lacking in moral clarity, ethically foggy. And mostly apathetic to the urgency in the world.

In college, I made sure to use the word "ambiguous" or "ambiguity" in every paper I wrote. So much was and is. It was, is eternally and specifically accurate in every context I care about.

About five years ago, I found the word "oscillate." Like to totter, wobble between things: Pain and healing. Sin and sorrow. Joy and anguish. Peace and restlessness. Passion and ambition. Me and you.

And now there is "beauty." I use the word too much, I suppose. But truly, it is the psalm of the season:

> One thing I ask of God, only that do I seek:
> to gaze upon the beauty of the Sacred One,
> all the days of my life.

I want to dwell in beauty all the time, sitting in my blue chair gazing out the window at the trees that respond so unequivocally to seasons. Walking down the block, looking at homes, and imagining the corners and angles and ceiling heights and the spaces of sanctuary. Talking to You, listening hard to what is said, to what is not said.

To dwell in beauty, to escape the pathetic, to rejoice in the ambiguity, to become unequivocal in my life's purpose and meaning.

To dwell in beauty, defined by the soft sweep of sacred that passes by my heart.

But if you need a synonym, try this:

Lovely.

Magnificent.

Sublime.

Or, as my mother began to say in the years before her death, Brilliant.

Choose one of these. Live there. Dwell there. Be there.

I Have Learned to Be Quiet

Learn to be quiet. You need not do anything.
Remain at your table and listen.
You need not even wait,
just learn to be quiet, still, and solitary.
And the world will freely offer itself to you unmasked.
It has no choice, it will roll in ecstasy at your feet.
                                                  —Franz Kafka

I LEARNED to be quiet at the edge of the creek.

And sometimes on a boulder not far from the creek's shore where the Maryland mica glistened as the sun was teaching me to be quiet. And the tall trees waving at the heavens, strong, and the woods so deep and traveled so far. And the path always softened by leaves and cracked acorns fallen this year or last, but soft and the earth and suitable support for my wandering spirit. And the sound of the creek dancing over the gentle ups and downs and the birds. The tough gawking crow, the light high-pitched sparrow, the robin calling, calling. An occasional bird of prey. Silent.

This is where I learned to be quiet and this is where my healing began, though I was only eight and then ten and then sixteen and there was so much hurt yet to be endured. And so much hurt that was already enduring.

But you learn the healing skill in the shadows of your youth, I think. Just as you learn the pain and insult of the bruised knee, the bruised heart, the free spirit that is made to shrink to fit in. But I didn't fit. And neither do you. We are as expansive as the wind in my woods that made the branches laugh with the sunlight as they played hide-and-seek. And we play hide-and-seek our entire life. We hide, God seeks.

God hides, we seek. We run, crouching low behind the trees waiting to be found, or stray a bit too far from the hill that will bring us back home. We giggle, we cry. We sit quietly watching, washing away the days, waiting to be found.

Still waiting to be found. And to find our way. And though I must have known, though I wouldn't have been able to say, it was the quiet I learned at the shores of my creek, or sometimes on the boulder near its shore, and often on the path that rambled miles and miles, that taught me about forgiveness. Though the sins were great, the beauty is even greater. And forgiveness is the only way home.

Maybe that is what is meant by return.

שִׁיר הַמַּעֲלוֹת מִמַּעֲמַקִּים קְרָאתִיךָ יְהֹוָה:
אֲדֹנָי שִׁמְעָה בְקוֹלִי תִּהְיֶינָה אָזְנֶיךָ קַשֻּׁבוֹת
לְקוֹל תַּחֲנוּנָי:

A song of ascents.
From the depths I call out to You:
Hear my voice;
Hear my supplications.

> —Psalm 130:1–2

Silence whistles in the open spaces.

> —Natan Alterman

The Story Is Told: The Turkey Prince

A tale by Rebbe Nachman of Bratzlav, perhaps written during one of his walks in the woods of the Ukraine, where he believed solitude was a salve for spiritual angst and dark wanderings. A tale about empathy, a tale about being lost and found. A tale of alienation and about the mad longing to claim our space at the royal table of divine closeness. It is a story that doesn't end. Our humanity is anchored in the perpetual longing to be recognized and accepted, to heal from the wounds of living, and the ever-present need to reach for a connection to holy and transcendent beauty. And so he teaches:

A PRINCE once became mad and thought that he was a turkey. He felt compelled to sit naked under the table, pecking at bones and pieces of bread, like a turkey. All the royal physicians gave up hope of curing him of this madness. The king grieved tremendously.

A sage arrived and said, "I will undertake to cure him." The sage undressed and sat naked under the table, next to the prince, pecking at crumbs and bones. "Who are you?" asked the prince. "What are you doing here?"

"And you?" replied the sage. "What are you doing here?"

"I am a turkey," said the prince.

"I'm also a turkey," answered the sage.

They sat together like this for some time until they became good friends.

One day, the sage signaled the king's servants to throw him shirts. He asked the prince, "What makes you think a turkey can't wear a shirt? You can wear a shirt and still be a turkey." With that, the two of them put on shirts. After a while, the sage again signaled, and they threw him pants. As before, he asked, "What makes you think that you can't be a turkey if you wear pants?" The sage continued in this manner until they were both completely dressed.

Then he signaled for regular food, from the table. The sage then asked the prince, "What makes you think you will stop being a turkey if you eat good food? You can eat whatever you want and still be a turkey!" They both ate the food.

Finally, the sage said, "What makes you think a turkey must sit under the table? Even a turkey can sit at the table."

The sage continued in this manner until the prince was completely cured.

—*Rebbe Nachman of Bratzlav*

Spiritual Companion

הֲיֵלְכוּ שְׁנַיִם יַחְדָּו בִּלְתִּי אִם־נוֹעָדוּ:

Can two walk together without having met? asks the prophet
Amos (3:3).

לְכוּ־נָא וְנִוָּכְחָה . . .

Come, let us consider together, answers Isaiah (1:18).

COME SIT by me. I have lost my words with all the noise and
rambling that abounds. So many opinions of who I should
be, nobody noticed that I crawled under the table. I pretend
to be satisfied, but I eat only crumbs. Somewhere, on the
way to responsibility, I lost myself. My youthful exuberance
diminished, somehow. Once I romped among fields of possibility, dreaming, playing roles to see what may fit. Shall I
be a firefighter, a ballerina, a general, a superhero, a painter?
Shall I save the world, invent the world, rule the world,
inspire the world, beautify the world, color outside the lines,
enforce the rules of order? I knew I could be anything.

And then somewhere in the rubble of should've, could've,
would've, I lost my words, walked away from the dreams,
left the table that was set for me before my birth. Abundant,
nourishing, a grandly set table.

One day, on the way to adulthood, I got up and sat on the
ground.

Come sit by me in silence. Not disinterested, distracted,
opinionated silence. A mindful silence feeling the tingle of
questions that are wandering, pondering. I won't go far if
you come sit by me.

Come sit by me, no judgment, only love. And curiosity. No thoughts, no conjectures, no telling me how or why, or because. Spiritual companion, just sit by me.

Bring me a sweater and jeans for when I get cold. I am vulnerable in the bare inquiry of who I am and what shall become of me. Beautiful self. Loving self. Love myself.

Bring me socks and shoes so that when I am ready, I can rise and stand firm. Set the table banquet-style. For I am regally awaiting to regain my place at the table.

As are you, by my side.

Be my spiritual companion, and I will be yours. We are all sages and princes, peasants and attendants to the crown.

Come sit by me, and I will sit by you.

Three Core Beliefs

THE TREES are about to change. They quiver in the air,
which is slowly thinning from hot to cool to cold.
And if we are to change, we ought to quiver as well.

Three essential beliefs are the heartbeat of days that are
holy, they are foundational to the essence of our humanity:

We are born with a pure heart.

Hate is senseless and destructive.

We have the capacity to choose, to change.

Four Practices: Change Your Destiny

*And Rabbi Yitzchak said: A person's sentence is torn up
on account of four types of actions. These are: Giving
charity, crying out in prayer, a change of one's name,
and a change of one's deeds for the better.*
—Babylonian Talmud, *Rosh HaShanah* 16b

*And to change their name, meaning to say "I am
someone else and I am not the same person who did
those things"; and to change all of their actions for good
and onto the straight path.*
—Maimonides, *Mishneh Torah*, Laws of Repentance 2:4

FOUR THINGS can change our destiny, said Rabbi Yitzchak
many centuries ago. I imagine him gazing at the midnight
sky abundant with stars and planets, pondering the constellation of things. How do we shift our destiny, he asked himself? Our days ricochet with that question. We walk upon a
path, clear and unclear, familiar yet alienating, affirming or
sometimes draining. How do we become better at being ourselves, realigning ourselves with good, with goodness, and
changing the constellation of things?

Late one night in the Israeli desert known as the Arava, I
lay down upon the earth for a long while. I watched the mil-
lions of stars that were watching me. A small group of people
were talking, sharing, and listening to music nearby. The
music was beautiful, spiritual, and celestial. I found myself
drawn to the heavens, deep in thought, far from fear, drawn
to the space between the land and the sky.

I asked to no one there, "How do I change my destiny?"
The answer came back from no one real, "Pray. Have an

active conversation with the Invisible. Sometimes with words, sometimes without. Sometimes, a cry. Shake your fists at the heavens if you'd like. Ask. Implore. Question."

"Show me the way," I said. "Unclench your fist," said the voice. "Reach out and open your hands. Generosity is redemption." I shifted my position, opening my hands, opening my heart.

"And then what?" I asked. "Change your name," she said. "Change how you walk through this world by humbly saying, *I am not the same person I once was.*"

And then he concluded sternly, "Distance yourself from the source of your trouble. Stay far away from trouble, troubled speech, troubled deeds, and those who draw you into trouble."

I lay there a little longer until my friend called me to go. As I arose, I was dizzy, disoriented, and lightheaded. These days can be difficult. They go deep and invite fundamental change.

Restoration

TIME, DISAPPOINTMENT, and hurt have dimmed
my inner light.

This light of my soul
this gift
from God
may be diminished
but has not gone out.

I shall do whatever I can to recover
even if it means letting go
of the darkness
that has been
my cover
for so long.

YOM KIPPUR

Gates, Books

I want a god who is like a window I can open
so I'll see the sky even when I am inside.
I want a god who is like a door that opens out, not in,
but God is like a revolving door, which turns, turns
*   on its hinges*
in and out, whirling and turning
without beginning, without end.
—Yehuda Amichai

The Book of Memory

My LIFE is a series of
comings and goings,
of twists and turns.

I tread upon the
struggles, difficulties,
and disappointments.

I walk the path of courageous living.
These cobblestones are uneven.

Tallit be my cape,
prayer be my secret source of power.

Heart be my wings.
I know who I am, I remember now.

I am beautiful.

A Humble Servant

טֶרֶם אֶעֱנֶה אֲנִי שֹׁגֵג וְעַתָּה אִמְרָתְךָ שָׁמָרְתִּי:
טוֹב־לִי כִי־עֻנֵּיתִי לְמַעַן אֶלְמַד חֻקֶּיךָ:

Before I was humbled, I went astray,
but now I keep Your word.
It was good for me that I was humbled,
so that I might learn Your laws.

—Psalm 119:67, 71

AFRAID, the prophet scrambled up a faraway mountain, hoping to hide. He came upon a cave seeking safety. An imposing Presence went to the mouth of the cave and whispered, *What are you doing here, Elijah?*

And the question lingers until today, heavy as the air of faith. What am I doing here? Who am I? And I am shaken by the wind, and cracked open by the quake, and singed by the fire. And still, the question.

Did you know that "humiliation" and "humility" are linguistic sisters and that "cumulus cloud" is a distant cousin? All are rendered from the same root, "flattened." On that imposing day centuries before, I imagine a cloud hovered in the distance, hinting, humbling. *What are you doing here, Elijah?* In the many answers that I will offer in my lifetime, I will oscillate between humiliation and humility until the day—maybe today—I will understand that it is I who chooses between the two.

And today, as the gates begin to close, I sing *Havdalah*, the prayer of separation, and I beckon Elijah and the question of the quest of the centuries.

What are you doing here?

I am here, I answer. Leveled and lowly. A humble servant of the highest good.

The Story Is Told: Before the Law

BEFORE THE LAW sits a gatekeeper. To this gatekeeper comes a man from the country who asks to gain entry into the law. But the gatekeeper says that he cannot grant him entry at the moment. The man thinks about it and then asks if he will be allowed to come in later on. "It is possible," says the gatekeeper, "but not now." At the moment the gate to the law stands open, as always, and the gatekeeper walks to the side, so the man bends over in order to see through the gate into the inside. When the gatekeeper notices that, he laughs and says, "If it tempts you so much, try it in spite of my prohibition. But take note: I am powerful. And I am only the most lowly gatekeeper. But from room to room stand gatekeepers, each more powerful than the other. I can't endure even one glimpse of the third."

The man from the country has not expected such difficulties: the law should always be accessible for everyone, he thinks, but as he now looks more closely at the gatekeeper in his fur coat, at his large pointed nose, and his long, thin, black, tattered beard, he decides that it would be better to wait until he gets permission to go inside. The gatekeeper gives him a stool and allows him to sit down at the side in front of the gate.

There he sits for days and years. He makes many attempts to be let in, and he wears the gatekeeper out with his requests. The gatekeeper often interrogates him briefly, questioning him about his homeland and many other things, but they are indifferent questions, the kind great men put, and at the end he always tells him once more that he cannot let him inside yet. The man, who has equipped himself with many things for his journey, spends everything, no matter how valuable, to win over the gatekeeper. The latter takes it all but, as he does so, says, "I am taking this only so that you do not think you have failed to do anything." During the many years the man observes the gatekeeper almost continuously. He forgets the other gatekeepers, and this one seems to him the only obstacle for entry into the law. He curses the unlucky circumstance, in the first years thoughtlessly and out loud, later, as he grows old, he still mumbles to himself. He becomes childish, and since in the long years studying the gatekeeper he has come to know the fleas in his fur collar, he even asks the fleas to help him persuade the gatekeeper.

Finally his eyesight grows weak, and he does not know whether things are really darker around him or whether his eyes are merely deceiving him. But he recognizes now in the darkness an illumination that breaks inextinguishably out of the gateway to the law. Now he no longer has much time to live. Before his death he gathers in his head all his experiences of the entire time up into one question that he has not yet put to the gatekeeper. He waves to him, since he can no longer lift up his stiffening body.

The gatekeeper has to bend way down to him, for the great difference has changed things to the disadvantage of the man. "What do you still want to know, then?" asks the gatekeeper. "You are insatiable."

"Everyone strives after the law," says the man, "so how is [it] that in these many years no one except me has requested entry?" The gatekeeper sees that the man is already dying and, in order to reach his diminishing sense of hearing, he shouts at him, "Here no one else can gain entry, since this entrance was assigned only to you. I'm going now to close it."

—*Franz Kafka*

The Shadows Fall

שְׂאוּ שְׁעָרִים רָאשֵׁיכֶם וּשְׂאוּ פִּתְחֵי עוֹלָם וְיָבֹא מֶלֶךְ הַכָּבוֹד׃

Lift my weary head to the eternal gates, lift me high that
the majesty of God may be ever present.

—Based on Psalm 24:9

ONCE AGAIN, the shadows fall. Let these be the shadows of
a day well spent in prayer and contemplation. Let them be a
sign of the day's end and not the shadows of my tired spirit.
We were born into goodness and have gone astray. *N'ilah.* We
come before the gates of prayer, the gates of repentance, the
barriers of our heart.

Is this a feeling of isolation, abandonment, or banishment?
Estrangement for sure. For many years we have formed an
armor that was supposed to protect us, and I suppose it did.
Until it didn't. It served us when we were tender. It protected
us and allowed us to build inner strength and resilience. Our
armor is the habits we have learned to wear. But we have been
saved from the cruelty that attacks innocence. Perhaps we no
longer need the shields and weapons of our youth . . .

Trust the strength and fortitude of your years. Rely on
the wisdom of passing time. What once cast us down to the
ground now offers a new pose. May we kneel on the holy
ground of humility. Forgiven. Forgiving.

And now as we search for the way back home, we must
ask—haven't our childhood protections stiffened us, dis-
tanced us, kept us sequestered rather than protected? Older,
stronger—aren't we ready to stand firm in vulnerability?

Less defensive, we can learn a new language. Less turbu-
lent, we can speak in softer tones. More open, may we speak
words of kindness and love.

I implore You, Source of mercy. I lay down my weapons, strip down, lower my armor. I stand at the gate of repentance, willing, forgiving, repentant. Open, open the gate, open with loving compassion. I bear no arms that can harm but only embrace. Open, open the gate. Open the gates of righteousness and I shall enter.

God of Records, God of Memory

נְדִי סָפַרְתָּה אָתָּה
שִׂימָה דִמְעָתִי בְנֹאדֶךָ
הֲלֹא בְּסִפְרָתֶךָ׃

You keep count of my wanderings,
put my tears into Your flask.
Are they not in Your book?

—Psalm 56:9

On Rosh HaShanah, it is written; on Yom Kippur, it is sealed.

—Un'taneh Tokef

THERE IS the Book of Life, and there is the Book of Death, and in between, the Book of Memory.

And in these books is the great drama of our lives, written with recurring themes of loss and love and anguish and joy and loneliness and belonging and passion and compassion and pain and healing.

And though the God of records is for me a metaphor, there is a permanence to what we have done, what was done to us, and who we have become. For what was will always be. Memories are living beings, sometimes living in our conscious mind, sometimes living in the unaware. Mostly warped and bent by time. Memory is not an accurate reporter. Remember returning to your childhood home? It was so much bigger then. And yet, memories form and inform. They are a record of sorts, referenced and considered.

I dance a tango with fate and destiny. *Who shall live and who shall die?*

Fate, the mysterious undertow, appears suddenly, pulling at us, making us struggle to stay afloat or not drift too far from the shore. Fate is beyond our doing. Larger than what we can know or understand. It is the playmate of the Unknown Forces that impose themselves upon our lives and our loves.

Who shall live and who shall die?

But our destiny unfolds from the fine threads of choices that are woven and knotted and stitched into the cloth that sets our table. Choice is the most powerful spiritual practice of all. We choose to react or not, to step forward or retreat; we choose to be angry for a very long time or not long enough; we choose to be positive and to fight the cynical view that we are not enough, don't have enough, will never be enough. Or not. We choose the company we keep; they reinforce our choices or enlighten us or challenge us or bore us and love us. Or not. Our destiny unfolds from the life we live, leaning toward righteousness, living in quiet contemplation, practicing generosity.

And through *t'shuvah*, return to the right path; through *t'filah*, prayer; through *tzedakah*, righteous living, fate's harshness can be softened.

These are days of memory, contemplating and analyzing, noticing and revealing how our fate and our destiny bump and bounce against each other and what we shall do about it. Fate and destiny are coauthors of the Book of Our Lives. We write the story by tending to what is within our control and releasing the rest to the mystery. Choosing to live a little better, a little kinder, a bit more forgiving, awake and aware.

*Rabbi Sh'muel bar Nachman said to Rabbi
Chanina bar Papa: The gates of prayer are
sometimes open and sometimes closed, but the
gates of repentance are always open.*
                              —D'varim Rabbah 2

*Prayer is like a mikveh, and repentance is like
the sea. The mikveh is sometimes open and
sometimes closed, just like the gates of prayer
are sometimes open and sometimes closed, but
the sea, the sea is always wide open, just like
the gates of repentance are open wide.*
                              —Eichah Rabbah 3

Eternity's Edge

A person should always view themselves as leaning
toward death. Death may find them at any time, even
in a state of sin. Therefore, they must always repent
and should not say, "When I grow older, I will repent."
For death may find them before they grow older. The
wise Solomon says, "At all times, your clothes should be
white" (Ecclesiastes 9:8).
    —Maimonides, *Mishneh Torah*, Laws of Repentance 7:2

THE MOMENT I truly see, know, and understand that I always live at eternity's edge, I am powerfully filled with life, a life that should be regarded with gentle purpose. I know my place is sacred yet fleeting. Always at the edge of eternity, I know my place is sacred yet fleeting. When we see, know, and understand that this life is but a moment, then we are gifted.

On the sands of the Mediterranean Sea, the shore is calm at twilight. Every setting sun, spectacular. There is a gentle play of white foam approaching, retreating, approaching, retreating, drawing near, withdrawing. Whenever possible, I spend my days there, in the presence of twilight, at the edge of the sea. I feel peace at the edge, the life force within every breath, every wave. Until one day, it's not. For what is a woman's life but a moment in time. This is my moment. My time. And yours.

I do not know where death will find me. But I know where life finds me. And you.

What a shift of perspective to live within the consciousness of our mortality rather than the delusion of immortality. That shift is a gift. For what are our days if not a command to live with grace and wonder and to be kind and humble? And what are these days, the High Holy Days, if not a reminder of our mortality? We don't like archaic words like "sin." But we do sin. And we don't understand the concept of repentance, but we must repent.

And when we are honest with ourselves, we know. We know so much when we pause in the silences and majesty of life.

The Ten Days of Repentance is an extended pause. We do not rise from the seat of contemplation until we are closer to knowing. Knowing who we are and the ripple effect of our behaviors. Knowing who we want to be and the unending power of love. Knowing not where death will find us. Knowing the constant play of the waves upon the sea and that every sunset is spectacular. Seeing, knowing, understanding this moment—this moment, this sacred moment.

Yom Kippur

Reckoning

Heaven can be reached
by those who weave with its blue,
walk on miracle as on stairs,
and know the way of the secret.
                    —Kadia Molodowsky

My Sacred Regard

THIS IS my spiritual reckoning, my sacred regard.

My reconciliation with the sun and moon and joy and tremendous beauty that surrounds me, entering into the crevasses even when my soul was weeping.

This is the moment when my sorrow is great, for I am sorry for so much. Though I do not regret my failures or the insults and assaults that come with living a life—I have been a faithful student of it all—I regret, so truly repent, the times that I was impatient, judgmental, and unkind. I am sorry.

And I am also delighted—lit up by the brightness of the world. Enlightened and infused by the light of my faith. And grateful. And now understand when my elders, some gone from sight, used to sigh and say, *I am blessed, I have been blessed in my life.* I understand the all-pervasive feeling of blessing. I understand the sigh.

I lean toward the mist of never more. I feel it in the balance of things and in my bones and blurred eyes, and in my ambitions, now quieter than ever before.

This is my call to the Invisible, the testament of my will, though not my last.

I will tarry in the days ahead, noticing it all. The pinches and the thrills. The noise and the song. The boredom and the fear. The prancing of youth and their unabashed desire to bend and break and disregard the rules that often constrict and confine. And the curiosity I hold so dear. And the creative gifts of my muse. And the God whispers. And the rock and roll of exuberance. And the wistful longing, my heart wistfully longs for beauty. And the quiet that comes with time.

For whatever time I have left, I continue to unfold in the wonder of it all.

Unfolding.

Sources and Permissions

Unless otherwise noted, translations from Hebrew texts are poetically rendered by the author.

Epigraph, vi. *All existence* . . . Rabbi Abraham Isaac Kook, *Abraham Isaac Kook: The Lights of Penitence, the Moral Principes, Lights of Holiness, Essays, Letters, and Poems*, trans. Ben Zion Bokser (Paulist Press, 1978), 381.

Introduction, xiii. *When I was young* . . . From Chayim Nachman Bialik, "The Pool," in *The Poetry of Kabbalah: Mystical Verse from the Jewish Tradition*, ed. and trans. Peter Cole and ed. Aminadav Dykman (Yale University Press, 2012), 246. Translated by the author.

Av: Humble Dust, Fertile Ashes, 1. *Comfort, comfort* . . . Translation from *The JPS Tanakh: Gender-Sensitive Edition* (Jewish Publication Society, 2023), found on Sefaria (sefaria.org).

Down to the Foundations, 3. *I am but dust* . . . *Sefer Kol Simchah: L'kutei Kol Simchah*, ed. Rabbi Alexander Zusha (Breslau, 1859), 123, as found on Hebrew Books, https://beta.hebrewbooks.org/10191.

The Story Is Told: Love Builds, Hate Destroys, 4. *Happy is the one* . . . Proverbs 28:14.

The Story Is Told: The Ruins of the Temple, 8. *Once, Rabbi Yochanan ben Zakkai* . . . Rabbi Solomon Schechter, ed., *Avot D'Rabbi Natan*, version A, chapter 4 (Vienna, 1887).

Acts of Love and Kindness, 9. *This was the place of holiness* . . . *Avot D'Rabbi Natan* 4:5.

Forty Days, 14. *Forty days* . . . Based on *Mishnah B'rurah* 581:1.

A Knock on the Door, 16. *Melissa Burkley* . . . Melissa Burkley, "The Hour Between Dog and Wolf," *Poets and Writers*, January/February 2019, 25–31. *In Rabbinic literature* . . . See Babylonian Talmud, *B'rachot* 9b.

Epigraph, 19. *When young Rabbi Eleazar of Koznitz* . . . Martin Buber, *Tales of the Hasidim: Later Masters* (Schocken Books, 1970), 177, adapted.

The Days of Awe and Terror, 20. *The line between* . . . "Ocean Vuong in Conversation with Mike Mills," August 6, 2023, in *City Arts & Lectures*, produced by City Arts & Lectures and KQED, podcast, https://www.cityarts.net/event/ocean-vuong-2/.

The Inner Life: *Cheshbon HaNefesh*, 23. *The King is in the field* . . . Alter Rebbe in his 1797 parable on the month of Elul, *Likutei Torah, Parashat R'eih*.

A Word, 25. *A person awakens . . .*
Sefer HaChinuch, mitzvah 606:2,
translated by Rabbi Francis
Nataf for Sefaria, 2018, found
on Sefaria (sefaria.org).

The Mystery: Prayer, God,
Silences, 33. *Bless me, my spirit*
. . . Rabbi Abraham Joshua
Heschel, "My Seal," in *The
Ineffable Name of God: Man*,
trans. Morton M. Leifman
(Continuum, 2007), 131.

The Unknown, 38. *Alone I sat . . .*
Quoted from *These Mountains:
Selected Poems of Rivka Miriam*,
translated by Linda Stern
Zisquit, 45, © 2009, The
Toby Press. Used with the
permission of Koren Publishers
Jerusalem Ltd. and The Toby
Press LLC.

Hannah's Prayer, 41. *She stood
alone . . .* Based on I Samuel
1:13.

Epigraph, 43. *When a person . . .*
Martin Buber, *Ten Rungs* (Cita-
del Press, 1995), 84, adapted.

Proclaim the Power of This
Day: *Un'taneh Tokef*, 48. *Let us
proclaim . . . Mishkan HaNefesh:
Machzor for the Days of Awe; Yom
Kippur* (CCAR Press, 2015),
212.

Hide and Seek, 52. *Hide and Seek*
. . . "Hide and Seek" from *God
Whispers: Stories of the Soul,
Lessons of the Heart* by Rabbi
Karyn D. Kedar (Jewish Lights/
Turner Publishing LLC, 1999),
25–27. Used by permission.
Adapted. *For the sin . . .* Trans-
lation from Reuven Hammer,

Entering the High Holidays: A
Complete Guide to the History,
Prayers, and Themes (Jewish
Publication Society, 1998), 137.

A Moment Ago, 54. *A moment ago*
. . . Rabbi Sheila Peltz Wein-
berg, *God Loves the Stranger:
Stories, Poems, Prayers* (White
River Press, 2017), 95.

The Story Is Told: The Whole
World Is Full of Glory, 55.
*Where is the dwelling place of
God* . . . Martin Buber, *Tales
of the Hasidim: Later Masters*
(Schocken, 1970), 277, adapted.
Where shall I find You . . . Judah
HaLevi, "Lord, Where Shall I
Find You?," in *A Penguin Book
of Hebrew Verse*, ed. and trans. T.
Carmi (Penguin, 1981), 338.

In Common, 56. *Each of us . . .*
Zelda, "Each of Us Has a
Name," in *The Spectacular
Difference: Selected Poems*,
trans. and ed. Marcia Lee
Falk (Hebrew Union College
Press, 2004), 141. *Tell me about
despair . . .* Mary Oliver, "Wild
Geese," in *Devotions: The Selected
Poems of Mary Oliver* (Penguin
Random House, 2017), 347.
Ask me to help . . . Inspired by
Josh Packard, John M. Vitek,
Ellen Koneck Mar, Jerry
Ruff, Josh Packard, PhD, and
Brian Singer-Towns, *Belonging:
Reconnecting America's Loneliest
Generation* (Springtide Research
Institute, 2020). There is "a
clear pattern in the stories of
young people as they moved
from joining a group to

ultimately experiencing true belonging within that group.... Over and over again, three distinct experiences showed up in their narratives: feeling noticed, feeling named, and feeling known" (62). Thank you to Rabbi Lily Goldstein for sharing this research.

Longing and Amazement, 64. *When I was young* . . . From Chayim Nachman Bialik, "The Pool," in *The Poetry of Kabbalah: Mystical Verse from the Jewish Tradition*, ed. and trans. Peter Cole and ed. Aminadav Dykman (Yale University Press, 2012), 246.

Epigraph, 65. *Religion consists of* . . . Rabbi Abraham Joshua Heschel, *I Asked for Wonder: A Spiritual Anthology*, ed. Samuel H. Dresner (Crossroads, 1983), 38. Adapted.

The Story Is Told: Lost and Found, 68. *Hanokh of Alexander* . . . Martin Buber, *Tales of the Hasidim: Later Masters* (Schocken Books, 1970), 314, excerpted from *The Classic Tales: 4,000 Years of Jewish Lore* by Ellen Frankel (Jason Aronson, 1993), 557. Used by permission of Rowman & Littlefield for Jason Aronson.

The Names of Rosh HaShanah, 69. *Keep me* . . . Rachel H. Korn, "Keep Hidden from Me," in *A Treasury of Yiddish Poetry*, ed. Irving Howe and Eliezer Greenberg, trans. Carolyn Kizer (Schocken Books, 1976),

306.

The Hidden Moon, 71. *Between Rosh HaShanah* . . . Translated from *The Metsudah Selichos*, trans. Rabbi Avrohom Davis (Metsudah Publications, 1986). License: CC-BY-SA, https://creativecommons.org/ licenses/by-sa/3.0/, found on Sefaria (sefaria.org). *This month shall mark* . . . Exodus 12:2 and Numbers 29:1.

The Story Is Told: Carry the Light Within, 72. *A young rabbi complained* . . . Martin Buber, *Tales of the Hasidim: Later Masters* (Schocken, 1970), 62–63, adapted.

HaYom Harat Olam: The Day Before the World Is Born, 73. *Today the world* . . . This anonymous prayer, titled in Hebrew as *HaYom Harat Olam*, first appeared in the ninth-century prayer book of Rav Amram of the Talmudic Academy in Sura, Persia (Iraq). This translation by Rabbi Sheldon Marder and Rabbi Janet Marder appears in *Mishkan HaNefesh: Machzor for the Days of Awe; Rosh HaShanah* (CCAR Press, 2015), 285.

Yom HaDin: The Day of Judgment, 75. *All of humanity* . . . Translated from the William Davidson digital edition of the *Koren Noé Talmud*, with commentary by Rabbi Adin Even-Israel Steinsaltz. License: CC-BY-NC, https:// creativecommons.org/ licenses/by-nc/4.0/, found on

Sefaria (sefaria.org).

Shofar: Breaking Through Complacency, 79. *Why* shofar *t'ruah* . . . Adapted from Daniel C. Matt, PhD, trans., *The Zohar: Pritzker Edition*, vol. 3 (Stanford University Press, 2005), as found in "Sounding the Shofar," in *Yovel: A Sourcebook for Fifty Years*, T'ruah, https://truah.org/wp-content/uploads/2017/03/Yovel-2-shofar.pdf.

Sh'varim: Sigh, 82. *One sage says* . . . Translation from the William Davidson digital edition of the *Koren Noé Talmud*, with commentary by Rabbi Adin Even-Israel Steinsaltz. License: CC-BY-NC, https://creativecommons.org/licenses/by-nc/4.0/, found on Sefaria (sefaria.org).

T'ruah: A Sad and Joyful Blast, 84. *Speak to the Israelite people* . . . Translation from *The Contemporary Torah: A Gender Sensitive Adaptation of the JPS Translation*, edited by David E. S. Stein, 2006 (license: CC-BY-SA; https://creativecommons.org/licenses/by/3.0/); found on Sefaria (sefaria.org). *A day of shofar song* . . . Leviticus 23:24 and 25:9, and Numbers 29:1. *Sing, sing* . . . Psalm 47:6. *The shofar shall arouse* . . . *Sefer HaChinuch* 405:2. *Happy are we* . . . Based on Psalm 89:16.

Epigraph, 86. *It sometimes happens* . . . Excerpts from *Abraham Isaac Kook: The Lights of Penitence, the Moral Principles, Lights of Holiness, Essays, Letters, and Poems* by Ben Zion Bokser; Copyright © 1978 by Ben Zion Bokser, published by Paulist Press, Inc. (paulistpress.com), 110. Used with permission.

The Ten Days of Repentance, 89. *How great is my inner struggle* . . . Excerpts from *Abraham Isaac Kook: The Lights of Penitence, the Moral Principles, Lights of Holiness, Essays, Letters, and Poems* by Ben Zion Bokser; Copyright © 1978 by Ben Zion Bokser, published by Paulist Press, Inc. (paulistpress.com), 377. Used with permission.

Lev Nishbar V'nidkeh: A Broken and Humbled Heart, 91. *Darkness covers* . . . Based on Psalm 51:19 and Proverbs 4:18.

Zero Visibility, 94. *Zero Visibility* . . . Excerpt from *The Bridge to Forgiveness: Stories and Prayers for Finding God and Restoring Wholeness* by Rabbi Karyn D. Kedar (Jewish Lights/Turner Publishing Company LLC, 2007), 132–33. Used by permission.

Returning Home, 103. *Three gifts* . . . Rabbi Jonathan Wittenberg, *The Eternal Journey: Meditations on the Jewish Year* (Aviv Press, 2004), 10.

Kol Nidrei, 105. *Kol Nidrei* . . . Kol Nidre/"The Sound of Pageantry: Willingness, Aspiration, and Discernment" by Rabbi Karyn D. Kedar from *All These Vows: Kol Nidre* by Rabbi

Larry Hoffman, PhD (Jewish Lights/Turner Publishing Company, 1998), 163–67. Used by permission. *With one voice . . . Mishkan HaNefesh: Machzor for the Days of Awe; Yom Kippur* (CCAR Press, 2015), 16. *All vows . . . Mishkan HaNefesh: Machzor for the Days of Awe; Yom Kippur* (CCAR Press, 2015), 18.

The Story Is Told: Repentance Is Healing, 108. *I will heal them . . .* Hosea 14:5. Translated from the William Davidson digital edition of the *Koren Noé Talmud*, with commentary by Rabbi Adin Even-Israel Steinsaltz. License: CC-BY-NC, https://creativecommons.org/licenses/by-nc/4.0/, found on Sefaria (sefaria.org).

Seven Practices Toward Awakening, 118. *Awake, awake you sleepers . . .* Translated by Eliyahu Touger (Moznaim, 1986). License: CC-BY-NC, https://creativecommons.org/licenses/by-nc/4.0/, found on Sefaria (sefaria.org).

The Paradox, 121. *Let us not be . . .* From the *Vidui* (Confession of Sin) liturgy of Yom Kippur. *I am grateful to You . . .* From *Modeh Ani* in the morning liturgy. *God, the soul You have given . . .* From *Elohai N'shamah* in the morning liturgy.

Confession, 124. *Confession . . .* Based on Song of Songs, chapters 4 and 5.

Draw Us Near, 126. *Happy are those . . .* Psalm 84:5–6.

The Story Is Told: Look for a New Way, 129. *Once our teacher . . .* S. Y. Agnon, *Days of Awe: A Treasury of Jewish Wisdom for Reflection, Repentance, and Renewal on the High Holy Days* (Schocken Books, 1948), 22, adapted. Copyright © 1948, 1965 by Penguin Random House LLC, copyright © 1975 by Penguin Random House LLC. Used by permission of Schocken Books, an imprint of the Knopf Doubleday Publishing Group, a division of Penguin Random House LLC. All rights reserved.

Three Sins, 132. *This is my favorite . . .* Rabbi Judith Z. Abrams, PhD, *Torah and Company: The Weekly Portion of Torah, Accompanied by Generous Helpings of Mishnah and Gemara, Served Up with Discussions Questions to Spice Up Your Sabbath Table* (Ben Yehuda Press, 2006), 51.

Forgive Me, 133. *Know that each and every . . .* Translation from *Likutei Moharan*, part II, 63:1, trans. Moshe Mykoff (Breslov Research Institute, 1986–2012). License: CC-BY-NC, https://creativecommons.org/licenses/by-nc/4.0/, found on Sefaria (sefaria.org).

The Story Is Told: Gossip, 135. *A certain person . . .* Based on the tale "A Bag of Feathers," attributed to Rabbi Levi Yitzchak of Berditchev, http://www.berdichev.org/a_bag_of_feathers.html.

What Can I Say?, 137. *What Can I Say?* . . . Based on Babylonian Talmud, *Arachin* 15b. *Gossip kills three people* . . . Babylonian Talmud, *Arachin* 15b. *Their tongue* . . . Jeremiah 9:7. Translated from the William Davidson digital edition of the *Koren Noé Talmud*, with commentary by Rabbi Adin Even-Israel Steinsaltz. License: CC-BY-NC, https://creativecommons.org/licenses/by-nc/4.0/, found on Sefaria (sefaria.org).

A Moral Compass, 144. *Who made the Pleiades* . . . Translation from *The JPS Tanakh: Gender-Sensitive Edition* (Jewish Publication Society, 2023), found on Sefaria (sefaria.org). *A sound is heard* . . . Isaiah 40:3.

Return to Love, 149. *In the morning I thought* . . . Zelda, "In the Morning I Thought," in *The Spectacular Difference: Selected Poems*, trans. and ed. Marcia Lee Falk (Hebrew Union College Press, 2004), 177.

Certain Words, 153. *One thing* . . . Psalm 27:4.

I Have Learned to Be Quiet, 155. *Learn to be quiet* . . . Attributed to Franz Kafka, found on a plaque when the author was wandering around Prague. The exact source is unknown and disputed by scholars, though most agree it is from his diaries.

Epigraph, 157. *Silence whistles* . . . Natan Alterman, *Selected Poems*, trans. Robert Friend (Hakibbutz Hameuchad, 1978), 17.

The Story Is Told: The Turkey Prince, 158. *A tale by Rebbe Nachman* . . . "Rebbi Nachman's Story—The Turkey Prince," Breslov Research Institute, May 31, 2009, https://breslov.org/rebbe-nachmans-story-the-turkey-prince/, with permission of the Breslov Institute.

Four Practices: Change Your Destiny, 163. *And Rabbi Yitzchak said* . . . Translated from the William Davidson digital edition of the *Koren Noé Talmud*, with commentary by Rabbi Adin Even-Israel Steinsaltz. License: CC-BY-NC, https://creativecommons.org/licenses/by-nc/4.0/, found on Sefaria (sefaria.org). *And to change their name* . . . Translated by Eliyahu Touger (Moznaim, 1986). License: CC-BY-NC, https://creativecommons.org/licenses/by-nc/4.0/, found on Sefaria (sefaria.org).

Gates, Books, 167. *I want a god* . . . *Open Closed Open: Poems by Yehuda Amichai* (Harcourt, 2000), 40. Compilation copyright © 2000 by Yehuda Amichai. English Translation Copyright © 2000 by Chana Bloch and Chana Kronfeld. Reprinted by permission of Georges Borchardt, Inc., on behalf of Chana Bloch, Chana Kronfeld, and the Estate of Yehuda Amichai.

A Humble Servant, 169. *Before I was humbled* . . . Translation of

Psalm 119 from *The JPS Tanakh* (Jewish Publication Society, 1985), found on Sefaria (sefaria. org).

The Story Is Told: Before the Law, 170. *Before the law* . . . Franz Kafka, "Before the Law," trans. Ian Johnston, Franz Kafka Online, https://www.kafka-online.info/before-the-law.html.

The Shadows Fall, 172. *N'ilah* is named for the closing of the gates—*n'ilat sh'arim*—of the Temple in Jerusalem (Babylonian Talmud, *Taanit* 26a). Today it serves as the closing service as the sun sets on Yom Kippur. *Open the gates of righteousness* . . . Psalm 118:9.

Epigraphs, 176. *Rabbi Sh'muel bar Nachman* . . . Translation from the Sefaria *Midrash Rabbah*, Sefaria Community Translation, found on Sefaria (sefaria. org). *Mikveh* . . . A mikveh is a ritual bathhouse. *Prayer is like a mikveh* . . . Translation from the Sefaria *Midrash Rabbah*, Sefaria Community Translation, found on Sefaria (sefaria.org).

Reckoning, 179. *Heaven can be reached* . . . Kadia Molodowsky, "And What Will Happen," trans. Jean Valentine, in *A Treasury of Yiddish Poetry*, ed. Irving Howe and Eliezer Greenberg (Schocken Books, 1976), 288. © All rights reserved to the authors and ACUM.

About the Author

RABBI KARYN D. KEDAR is an author, poet, and inspirational speaker renowned for her honest and passionate approach to mindfulness, healing, and the deeper aspects of the human experience. She writes and teaches on themes such as forgiveness, beauty, struggle, and love, offering insight and guidance to people of all faiths, as well as those seeking deeper meaning in their lives.

In addition to her writing, Rabbi Kedar is a sought-after keynote speaker, lecturer, and workshop leader, engaging communities across the country and bringing her insights to life in powerful and meaningful ways. Her previous works, including *Amen: Seeking Presence with Prayer, Poetry, and Mindfulness Practice* and *Omer: A Counting* (both published by CCAR Press), have been praised for their thoughtfulness, clarity, and ability to touch the human spirit.

Rabbi Kedar's philosophy is beautifully expressed in her own words: "Every morning that we are granted another day of life, we are invited to the miracle of awakening. Come to the edge of what you know and sit awhile. Find the courage to live fearlessly; to emerge and unfold; to create a life of meaning and purpose."

Rabbi Kedar lives with her husband Ezra just outside of Chicago, Illinois. Their children and six grandchildren continue to make their way in both Israel and the United States.

Rabbi Kedar is available for readings, lectures, and retreats. Contact her at karynkedar.com or use the QR code to be directed to her website.

www.ingramcontent.com/pod-product-compliance
Lightning Source LLC
Chambersburg PA
CBHW070329090426
42733CB00012B/2418